Hamel

Other Books by John Laffin

MILITARY

Brassey's Battles (3500 Years of Conflict)

War Annual 1 *through* 8

Middle East Journey

Return to Glory

One Man's War

The Walking Wounded

Digger (The Story of the Australian Soldier)

Scotland the Brave (The Story of the Scottish Soldier)

Tommy Atkins (The story of the English Soldier)

Jackboot (The Story of the German Soldier)

Jack Tar (The Story of the English Seaman)

Swifter Than Eagles (Biography of Marshal of the Royal Air Force Sir John Salmond)

The Face of War

British Campaign Medals

Codes and Ciphers

Boys in Battle

Women in Battle

Anzacs at War

Links of Leadership

Surgeons in the Field

Americans in Battle

Letters From the Front 1914-18

The French Foreign Legion

Damn the Dardanelles! (The Agony of Gallipoli)

The Australian Army at War 1899-1975

The Arab Armies of the Middle East Wars 1948-1973

The Israeli Army in the Middle East Wars 1948-1973

Fight for the Falklands!

On the Western Front: Soldiers' Stories 1914-18

The War of Desperation: Lebanon 1982-85

The Man the Nazis Couldn't Catch

Battlefield Archaeology

Holy War (Islam Fights)

Western Front 1916-17: The Price of Honour

Western Front 1917-18: The Cost of Victory

World War I in Postcards

Soldiers of Scotland (with John Baynes)

Greece, Crete & Syria 1941

Secret and Special (Australian Operations)

British Butchers & Bunglers of World War I

The World in Conflict

Western Front Illustrated

Guide to Australian Battlefields of the Western Front

Panorama of the Western Front

Western Front Companion

Digging Up the Diggers' War

We Will Remember Them: AIF Epitaphs of World War I

Brassey's Book of Espionage

Gallipoli

The Somme

Raiders: The Great Exploits of World War II

Hamel: The Australians' Greatest Victory

Guide to the Australian Battlefields of the Western Front

GENERAL

The Hunger to Come
(Food and Population Crises)

New Geography 1966-67

New Geography 1968-69

New Geography 1970-71

Anatomy of Captivity (Political Prisoners)

Devil's Goad

Fedayeen (The Arab-Israeli Dilemma)

The Arab Mind

The Israeli Mind

The Dagger of Islam

The Arabs as Master Slavers

The PLO Connections

Know the Middle East

Fontana Dictionary of Africa Since 1960
(With John Grace)

Hitler Warned Us

Aussie Guide to Britain

The Spirit and the Source: A Poet and his Inspiration

A Kind of Immortality

and other titles, including novels

THE BATTLE OF
HAMEL

THE AUSTRALIANS' FINEST VICTORY

John Laffin

Kangaroo Press

First published in Australia in 1999 by Kangaroo Press
an imprint of Simon & Schuster (Australia) Pty Limited
20 Barcoo Street, East Roseville NSW 2069

A Viacom Company
Sydney New York London Toronto Tokyo Singapore

National Library of Australia
Cataloguing-in-Publication data

Laffin, John. 1922-

The battle of Hamel: the Australian's Finest Victory

Includes index.
ISBN 0 86417 970 7.
1. Le Hamel (France), Battle of, 1918. 2. World War, 1914-1918 - Campaigns -
France. 3. World War, 1914-1918 - Participation, Australian. I. Title

940.434

Set in Goudy 10.7/14.5
Printed by the Australian Print Group, Maryborough

10 9 8 7 6 5 4 3 2

Georges Clemenceau, Prime Minister of France addressing Australian soldiers on 7 July 1918

When the Australians came to France, the French people expected a great deal of you. We knew that you would fight a real fight but we did not know that from the very beginning you would astonish the whole continent. I shall go back and say to my countrymen — 'I have seen the Australians, I have looked in their faces. I know that these men will fight alongside of us again, until the cause for which we are fighting is safe for us and for our children.'

Clemenceau's audience consisted, in part, of Diggers who had won the Battle of Hamel three days earlier.

This book is dedicated to the Diggers of Hamel and through them to the Australian Corps of 1918 and their leader, Lieutenant General Sir John Monash.

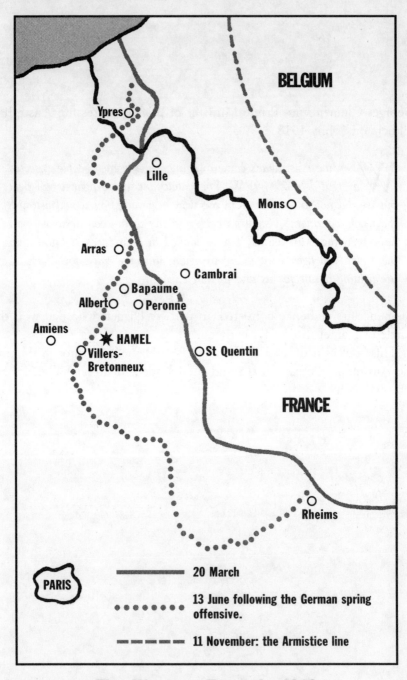

The Western Front in 1918

BELGIUM

Ypres

Lille

Mons

Arras

Cambrai

Bapaume

Albert

Peronne

Amiens

★ HAMEL

Villers-
Bretonneux

St Quentin

FRANCE

Rheims

PARIS

———— 20 March

•••••••• 13 June following the German spring
offensive.

– – – – 11 November: the Armistice line

Contents

Author's Note 8
Abbreviations 10

1. The Great Discovery *11*
2. The Prelude: 1914–15 *18*
3. The Impotence of Australian Command *25*
4. Fromelles: How to Lose a Battle *33*
5. Gaining Fame, Losing Men *44*
6. Preparations for Battle *54*
7. Into Battle *71*
8. The Feint Attack North of the Somme *87*
9. The German Counterattack *94*
10. High Spirits; Sad Episodes *101*
11. The Wounded; the Tanks; the Americans; Aeroplanes *107*
12. Congratulations All Round and Suggestions for Monash *126*
13. The Rare Process of Analysing Success *135*
14. Australian Corps Memorial Park *143*

Postscript 150
Appendix I: A Battalion Order for Battle 151
Appendix II: Battle of Hamel Board of Enquiry 154
Appendix III: Rewriting History 157
Appendix IV: 'Ninety-Three Minutes in the History of the World' 162
Glossary 165
General Index 169
Index of Military Units 175

Author's Note

Writing the story of the Battle of Hamel is the fulfilment of an intellectual and emotional experience that began in 1960. In the period between 1960 and 1999 I wrote more than a hundred books and while all were satisfying to bring to print, none was more so than *Hamel*. History has shamefully neglected this battle, in which Australian independent military leadership matured. I have tried to make amends.

My wife Hazelle and I for thirty-seven years waged a campaign to have this remarkable battle adequately remembered. Not until the arrival in 1996 of Bruce Scott as Minister for Veterans' Affairs did proposals take shape. Somebody in political authority had to give approval and Bruce did so. Perhaps we are all fortunate that the father and grandfather of Prime Minister John Howard served at Hamel, because he supported his minister's intentions.

Among the people I wish to thank for their assistance are Air Vice-Marshal Alan Heggen, when he was Director of the Office of Australian War Graves, Ian Cartwright, his deputy, and Peter Burness of the Australian War Memorial. The person principally responsible for physically bringing the Australian Corps Memorial Park of Hamel into being on the ground was Brigadier Kevin O'Brien, who had been appointed by Office of Australian War Graves as project co-ordinator. He is mentioned elsewhere in the book.

In writing this book I have been greatly helped by the *Official History of Australia in the War of 1914–1918*, volume VI, by C. E. W. Bean. Every historian who has ever written about the First World War must of necessity consult Bean's prodigious work. Any future historian of that war will need Bean's volumes by his side.

I have also made use of *Jacka's Mob* by E. J. Rule, who fought at Hamel. In 1985 Dr Peter Pedersen wrote a brilliant history of John Monash, *Monash as a Military Commander*. This deeply researched book was of great help to me. In *The Burford Sampson Great War Diary*, published privately in 1997 by his son, Richard, I found interesting comments and observations about the battle, during which Sampson was a major in the 15th Battalion.

Other books consulted include:

Brahms, V., *The Spirit of the Forty-Second*, Brisbane, 1938.
Cutlack, F. M., *The Australians: Their Final Campaign 1918*, London, 1918 (I discussed Hamel with Freddy Cutlack in the 1960s).

Liddell Hart, B. H., *The Tanks*, vol. 1, London, 1949.

Maurice, F., *The Life of General Lord Rawlinson of Trent*, London, 1928.

Serle, Geoffrey, *John Monash: a Biography*, Melbourne 1982.

Taylor, A. J. P., *The First World War*, Ringwood, 1972.

Wanliss, N. F., *The History of the Fourteenth Battalion AIF*, Melbourne, 1929.

White, T. A., *The Fighting Thirteenth*, Sydney, 1924.

I also consulted numerous personal diaries, letters, unit histories, war diaries, and other contemporary documents held in the Research Department of the Australian War Memorial, whose staff were invariably helpful.

I am often surprised how many soldiers other than officers kept diaries or wrote spontaneous descriptions of the events in which they played a part. Their observations are always interesting and sometimes graphic. It is intriguing to note that the men were well informed about what was happening. This indicates that officers took them into their confidence, a notable feature of life in the AIF. Inevitably, the writers were not always accurate because a battle is confusing and it is only later that the many and varied actions within an operation can be put into sequence and perspective.

We are fortunate that officers of the American 33rd Division, small parts of which supported the Australians in the battle, reported to their HQ in such detail. I have studied all these reports and have made much use of them. Colonel J. B. Sanborn, CO of the 131st Infantry Regiment, and Colonel Abel Davis, CO of the 132nd Infantry Regiment, each wrote narratives of the battle. Both colonels had platoons of soldiers engaged in the Hamel fighting and their narratives are as detailed as anything that C. E. W. Bean wrote, though shorter. Bean quotes from the American reports in his *Official History*.

Finally, my thanks to Chantal Persyn for so professionally typing my work onto computer disk, and to Anny De Decker for other work in the preparation of this book.

Considering the depth and quality of my sources, if there are any errors they are mine alone.

John Laffin
November 1998

Abbreviations

ADS Advanced dressing station

AEF American Expeditionary Force

AFC Australian Flying Corps

AIF Australian Imperial Force

ANZAC Australian and New Zealand Army Corps; also, as Anzac, the name given to the Australian sector at Gallipoli and to a veteran of the Anzac campaign

BEF British Expeditionary Force

Bn Battalion

CO Commanding Officer (of a battalion, usually a lieutenant colonel)

Cpl Corporal

CSM Company Sergeant Major

DCM Distinguished Conduct Medal

Div. Division

DSO Distinguished Service Order

FOO Forward observation officer (for artillery)

GHQ General Headquarters (of the entire army)

GOC General officer commanding (of a brigade, division or corps)

HE High explosive

HQ Headquarters (generally referring to a battalion)

IO Intelligence officer

L/cpl Lance corporal

MC Military Cross

MG Machine-gun

MM Military Medal

MO Medical officer

NCO Non-commissioned officer

OC Officer Commanding (of a company)

ORs Other ranks

RAP Regimental aid post

RSM Regimental sergeant major

SAA Small arms ammunition

Sgt Sergeant

VC Victoria Cross

CHAPTER 1

The Great Discovery

During the hot summer of 1960 my wife Hazelle and I were once again exploring Australian battlefields of the First World War. We had already visited Gallipoli and the Sinai Desert of Palestine and we had been active on the Western Front of France and Flanders since the beginning of 1956.

Australian soldiers — the Diggers — had been active on these battlefields between April 1916 and November 1918, when the war ended. Their service was outstanding, their sacrifice immense and their achievements remarkable. We were following in their footsteps, from one campaign to the next, walking across the old battlegrounds, visiting their crowded military cemeteries, tracing their camping grounds and billets. We would do this for the next forty years but what we found that 4 July 1960 was one of our most important discoveries.

We had wanted to locate Australian trenches but this proved difficult. The combatant armies had dug thousands of miles of trenches between 1914 and 1918 but most had long since been ploughed over and returned to farmland, fields and forests. Great areas were covered by industrial developments, housing estates and office complexes while other former trench areas had been obliterated by broad motorways. Long stretches of the north–south motorways of France by coincidence closely followed the line of the Western Front as it was in 1917. Decade by decade, the former killing fields had disappeared, from Nieuport in Belgium at the northern end of the Western Front to Belfort on the Swiss border at its southern extremity.

The Australians had fought in certain areas of that 500-kilometre front, notably in Belgian and French Flanders, which included the Ypres Salient, to some extent in the *département* of the Nord, famously in the *département* of the Somme and, in the closing months of the war, in the Aisne.

The trench systems were complex, with front, support and reserve trenches, as well as communication trenches linking all three. As the fortunes of war flowed and ebbed, with armies advancing and retreating, so troops had to dig-in again, creating yet other lines of defence. From 1915 onwards the entire war was fought to capture trenches and always with a terrible cost in lives.

In theory, considering the intensive service of the Australian Imperial Force (AIF) there should still be some trenches extant where the Diggers had found shelter from the storm of enemy shells and bullets and from where they launched their attacks against the occupying German armies.

Indeed, in several places we did find trenches, by now eroded and weathered, but then came the problem of proving them to have been used by Australian soldiers. The British, the Canadians, New Zealanders, South Africans and Belgians had also fought in some of the same sectors as the Diggers. The French Army, by far the largest on the Allied side, had its long special parts of the front, but on occasions they too occupied trenches in the regions that had generally been defended by France's allies.

Exploring the low, scrubby hills east of the small village of Le Hamel, just south of the Somme River and close to Villers-Bretonneux, I speculated that they could have been held by Australian units. We found rusty steel helmets, battered waterbottles now without their original felt covering, even some twisted rifles but all the British Empire armies had used the same equipment. While the AIF had seen significant service at Le Hamel, the relics we found could not possibly identify the nationality of the troops who had used them. An added complication was that in the Le Hamel trench line we came across the remains of a standard French Lebel rifle as well as other indications that the *poilus* had been there. (French front-line soldiers were known as poilus — 'hairy ones'.) Further, we found some German Mauser rifle cartridge cases and the remnants of a German gas respirator.

We searched the area for some days and carried out random archaeological digs but still found nothing that was definitively Australian, such as badges and buttons. Yet... the Diggers had captured Le Hamel from the Germans on 4 July 1918 and then pushed their enemies up and over these hills. It was reasonable to assume that they had taken over the enemy trenches and then worked at turning them round against their former occupants, known to the Diggers as Huns, Jerries or Fritzes. 'Turning them round' is actually what happened because trenches have a front, with the parapet, and a rear, the parados. The German parados was now made into the stronger parapet. It was obvious to me in 1960 that this had happened, but weathering in later years reduced front and rear lips of the trenches to equal proportions.

These trenches were probably Australian and a certain roughly circular position nearby, known during the war as the Wolfsberg, would have been turned into an AIF forward post. History often deals with probables, but when this happens endless arguments ensue. Sceptics come forward to say, 'There is another possibility...' Among the many people who take a keen and active interest in the Great War on the Western Front are some who resent the publicity given to the Australians during the war — and even at the end of the twentieth century. They would be bound to contest any Australian claim to ownership of the Le Hamel trenches unless proof of occupancy could be produced.

The truth lay in the official trench maps produced by army survey companies during the war. These meticulously drawn maps were revised from time to time and frequently so when trenches were won or lost. I always use trench maps when exploring the Western Front and I have one, owned by Staff Captain Hale of the 5th Brigade, which clearly shows Australian units holding the Hamel line of trenches up to 8 August 1918. From these same trenches the Diggers that day 'hopped the bags' — as they described jumping over the parapet — to begin the great Allied offensive which was to culminate three months later in the German surrender and the consequent Armistice. We already knew that the AIF had captured the trenches; now we knew that they had held them until the grand assault began. Captain Hale's trench map was the proof.

Other nations had created splendid memorial parks to commemorate the war service of their men and their terrible sacrifice. The Canadians were first off the mark after the war with their domain on Vimy Ridge. Even little Newfoundland, then separate from Canada, which did not have the manpower to contribute more than a single regiment to the British effort, had a large and impressive memorial park at Beaumont-Hamel (no connection with Le Hamel). The 'Newfies' had a special reason for their memorial to be sited at Beaumont-Hamel. Here, early in the Battle of the Somme, July 1916, their regiment had been wiped out as the soldiers advanced in their attack. The South Africans claimed Delville Wood, east of Albert, as their own, for the very good reason that the South African Brigade suffered grievous losses during six days of bloody battle, also in July 1916. In the middle of the wood, they have built a colonial-type fort as their national memorial.

The British asked Sir Edwin Lutyens to design a memorial on the heights above the Ancre River and he created the Thiepval Memorial, which can be seen for many miles around. It, too, is generously provided with parkland.

The Australians were not inactive. They were building memorials on the Western Front even before the war ended, one for each of the five AIF Divisions. They were erected at sites chosen by the former leaders of the divisions as places significant for the divisions' service and sacrifice. The 1st Division has its memorial at Pozières, the 2nd at Mont St Quentin, near Péronne, the 3rd at Sailly-le-Sec, on the Somme, the 4th at Bellenglise, close to the old German Hindenburg Line, the 5th in Polygon Wood, Ypres (now Ieper). The 2nd Division has another memorial at Pozières. There is also an Australian National Memorial in the grounds of the military cemetery at Villers-Bretonneux.

However, successive Australian governments appeared to lack the vision to create an AIF memorial park, despite the precedent set by Canada. Yet Canada and Australia suffered roughly equal losses during the war — more than 60 000 men killed and 150 000 wounded. Canada's advantage was that one of its citizens was the newspaper magnate Lord Beaverbrook, who was instrumental in the acquisition of French land for a park and in creating a fitting memorial. Both the Canadian and the Newfoundland parks retained the thousands of shellholes and long lengths of trench, and around them their respective parks took shape. The Canadian memorial park incorporates the tunnels dug by soldiers as a preliminary to the Battle of Vimy Ridge, 9 April 1917, the Canadians' most impressive victory.

Having found the Australian trenches at Le Hamel, Hazelle and I saw at once that this was the place for an Australian memorial park and that it could serve the double purpose of commemorating the Australian Corps and its remarkable victory at Le Hamel. It was the Australians' finest triumph — though by no means their greatest battle — and it had the added distinction of having set a pattern for Allied victory for the final months of the war.

Convincing the authorities that such a memorial was not only desirable but also essential to give the Australian nation its due credit among the former Allies who had ended Germany's ruinous aggression against its neighbours was much more difficult than locating the trenches.

In turn, I approached a governor-general, and four prime ministers, as well as numerous leaders of Australian ex-servicemen's organisations, various politicians and church leaders. Nearly all said, in effect, 'What a great idea. Let us see what we can do about it'. However, the politicians, from prime ministers down to lowly backbenchers, saw no votes in a new type of memorial 12 000 miles from home.

Sir Robert Menzies in retirement gave me strong moral support and told me he would refer my suggestion to certain of his former ministers. I expected his support because in the 1951 federal elections, at his direct personal request, I had stood for federal parliament in a hopeless seat. I have no proof that he ever did use his prestige to influence his successors and ministers of the day.

In several of my books I urged the need for an AIF memorial park but it was not until the appointment of Air Vice-Marshal (retd) Alan Heggen as Director of the Office of Australian War Graves and the selection of Bruce Scott as Minister for Veterans Affairs that positive interest was taken, and then definite action.

In 1993 Colonel (now Brigadier) Kevin O'Brien, of Australian Army Training Command, produced a film about the Battle of Le Hamel. I was the military adviser and the on-screen presenter for the film, which was called *The Fighting Spirit: The Battle of Hamel, the Turning Point*. It was shot almost entirely on the old battleground and then combined with archival footage. It proved immensely successful and at last the Australian public could see what was so very important about this particular battle.

Despite its brilliance, the victory at Le Hamel had been almost totally obscured by the drama and the terrible losses in men of the Battles of Fromelles, Pozières, Passchendaele, Messines, Villers-Bretonneux, Bullecourt and Mont St Quentin-Péronne. I am not being cynical when

I say that, for generations of Australians stupefied and shocked by the blood-letting on the killing fields of the Great War, not enough blood was spilled at Le Hamel to make the battle noteworthy. And how could an operation which had lasted such a short time — only ninety-three minutes — be as 'important' as, say, the First Battle of the Somme, which had ground on with unabated ferocity for five-and-a-half months, producing one million casualties?

This book tells the story of the Battle of Hamel, which was revolutionary at the time in its tactics. But first I describe the strategy, the tactics and the top-level leadership during the four years before the action at Le Hamel. The strength and resilience of the German enemy are important, as are the nature and skill of the Australians who took part in the operation. Of special importance is the role of the small numbers of Americans supporting the Diggers.

Above all, I am concerned with the planning and operational management of this remarkable battle. It was the Australians' first experience, in four years, of fighting entirely under their own commanders, who had masterminded the operation from start to finish. Above all, it was with Le Hamel that Australian military leadership came to confident maturity. Historically, it is tragic that this maturity was given no opportunity to manifest itself two years earlier.

Finally, I explain why Le Hamel was a great turning point of the war. It established the model for subsequent operations. The Diggers made history when they used their captured trenches as the springboard from which, with the Canadians, they brilliantly spearheaded the Allied advance on 8 August 1918.

At the end, I describe the several features of the new Australian Battlefield Memorial Park which make it the equal of the Canadian park, which for so long had no equal in the excellence of its presentation.

On 4 July 1998 historic justice was at long last done to the Australian Corps and its commander-in-chief, Lieutenant General Sir John Monash. The Australian Corps Memorial Park and the memorial itself were opened by Ian McLachlan, Minister of Defence, and Bruce Scott. McLachlan's name takes precedence on the plaque because his Ministry is senior to that of Scott for Veteran's Affairs.

✦ ✦ ✦

The *Australian Official History of the Great War*, trench maps, newspaper reports and soldiers' memoirs, including those of John Monash himself, refer to the village where the battle took place, and the action itself, as Hamel, not Le Hamel. After Chapter 1, I conform to this practice. The Australians of the earlier era had no idea that the French name was Le Hamel and, strictly speaking, not even 'Le' but 'le'.

One of the many British officers sent to AIF HQ to study the spectacular success of the Hamel operation was an obscure brigadier, Bernard Montgomery. He was to become Field Marshal Montgomery, the victor of El Alamein in 1942 and one of the great leaders of the Allied invasion of Europe to end the Nazi occupation in 1945. From Montgomery's tactics it is easy to see that he was influenced by what he learnt from Monash and his officers.

CHAPTER 2
The Prelude: 1914–15

The European war which broke out in August 1914 was an act of collective political madness. It is essential to know something of the sort of war into which the Australian government committed the nation and its soldiers. This explanation is necessary to make clear how a small nation of only 4 000 000 people could lose more than 60 000 servicemen killed and at least 150 000 wounded.

To Australians these were appalling losses and eighty years later they are still considered in these terms. It has to be stressed that for Europeans such a butcher's bill was minute compared to their nations' losses. This is why, in the 1990s, French, British, Germans and Russians could say to me, in genuine surprise, 'Australia lost only sixty thousand men killed! It got off lightly'.

European politics did not attract much attention in Australia in 1914. What mattered most was the price of the primary products which Australia exported to Europe, particularly to Great Britain. When war broke out in August the news at first evoked only muted alarm in Australia.

In Europe, political and military leaders on both sides of the conflict confidently predicted that it would not last long. After all, they all knew that God was with them. The Germans, with their allies, the Austrian–Hungarian Empire, were so sure of His aid that every German soldier's waistbelt buckle carried the prominent words 'Gott mit uns' (God with us).

The French, British and Belgian allies were equally confident of victory, if only because they had moral right on their side, and God favoured the righteous, didn't He? Germany was demonstrably the aggressor and deserved to lose. Church leaders in the Entente countries assured their peoples that God fought with them. The French might once have taken some comfort from Napoleon's maxim that 'God is on the side of the big battalions', but in 1914 Germany had the largest armies. The German

High Command had learnt a great deal from Napoleon. The Russians, allied with Britain, France and Belgium, were also under attack by the Germans and from their sanctuary of the Orthodox Church they too claimed divine support. God was being forced to take sides.

Britain had a splendidly trained regular army of only 100 000 but the people wanted to believe their leaders' assurances that the war would be over by Christmas — and they meant Christmas 1914. It would be a short but heroic war. The British would do their share but they were counting on French military manpower, which far exceeded that of the British.

In their tens of thousands, young men of the belligerent countries flocked to join the colours. The British dominions were enthusiastic about the war — or at least their leaders were. Australia declared its willingness to join the British and Allied cause and on the eve of the war Andrew Fisher, who was then the leader of the opposition, pledged support 'to the last man and the last shilling'. This was one of the most astonishing examples of patriotic hyperbole in a war noted for overstatement. It was also ingenuous, politically immature and an unwarrantable assumption that he had the right to commit the nation's men to annihilation, should that prove necessary. By September, however, Fisher was prime minister.

If the numbers of men and the size of armies could have had any bearing on the duration of the war, it should indeed have been over by Christmas. But the greater the size of armies involved in any war, the more the likelihood of lengthy stalemate.

At the beginning of the war, the Germans appeared to be on the verge of breakthrough. The Schlieffen Plan, a masterly manoeuvre which the German General Staff had long before prepared for their invasion of Belgium and France, at first succeeded, but the great forces of Germany and France were roughly equal in strength and no real penetration occurred.

Australians of the 1914–15 period knew little about the battles being fought on the Western Front before their soldiers arrived in France from Gallipoli. Had they known, they might not have been so eager to commit their young men to the inferno. In brief outline these are some of the battles:

Battle of the Frontiers of France, 20–24 August 1914.
This was a gigantic prelude to what came to be called The Great War. The five-day battle stretched from the Swiss border in the south to Mons,

in Belgium, in the north. The Germans committed seven armies, the French five and the British one, of about 70 000 men. The total number of troops involved was more than 3 000 000. The segments of the battle consisted of the Battles of Lorraine, Ardennes, Sambre (also called Charleroi) and Mons.

The result was a resounding defeat for the French and British. The French, with 1 250 000 men involved, suffered 300 000 casualties, the Germans about the same. At Mons the British had 4244 casualties in holding up the German advance for nine hours.

Le Cateau, 26 August 1915.
The British Army's biggest battle since Waterloo in 1815. General Smith-Dorrien, commanding XI Corps during the retreat from Mons, blocked the onrushing Germans for eleven hours, thus enabling the British Expeditionary Force (BEF) to escape from the great German sweep. The corps, of three-and-a-half divisions, lost 8077 men and thirty-six guns.

First Battle of Ypres (now Ieper), 14 October–11 November 1914.
In the very first quarter of the conflict, this battle set the pattern for what was to follow. Ypres, in Belgian Flanders, and the slightly higher ground to its east was a key point in the Allied Western Front, with the Belgian Army holding the line from Ypres to the North Sea and the British from Ypres south to La Bassée. The German chief-of-staff, von Falkenhayn, attacked with the Fourth and Sixth Armies on 14 October. Weak in military strength but strong in resolution, the Belgians could hold their front only by opening sea sluicegates and flooding the flat country. The French rushed in massive reinforcements during the nine-day German offensive, then General Foch launched a great but vain counterattack, 20–28 October.

At Ypres, the British had clung to a salient that poked ten kilometres into the German front and could not be dislodged before heavy rain and snow ended the battle. The brave but foolish assaults against massed artillery and machine-gun fire caused enormous casualties. German, 130 000; French, 50 000; British, 2368 officers and 55 787 men; Belgian, 32 000.

First Battle of the Marne River, 6–8 September 1914
This battle raged along a 300-mile front, with attacks and counterattacks.

General Moltke called off the German offensive on 9 September and the entire German line began a forty-mile fighting withdrawal to the Aisne River. Moltke lost his job and was replaced by von Falkenhayn. The British Army was the only Allied force which advanced continuously through 5–8 September and the only army to cross the Marne before the German retreat. With only 70 000 effective troops — 11 032 had become casualties at Mons and Le Cateau — the British had achieved more than could be expected of them. To this vast battle, the Germans committed forty-four infantry and seven cavalry divisions — 900 000 men; the French–British allies, fifty-six infantry and nine cavalry divisions — 1 082 000 men. The casualties were in proportion. The French lost about 250 000, the Germans 200 000. In both cases detailed figures were never published.

Champagne Campaigns, 20 December 1914–17 March 1915
In the depths of winter, the French lost many men in vain attacks against German machine-guns. On 25 September, apparently having learned nothing from the earlier fighting, General Joffre launched another attack under Generals Pétain and Le Cary and actually captured 32 000 enemy troops and 150 guns. But to achieve this 'victory' the French suffered 145 000 casualties and both sides held their original positions.

Neuve-Chapelle, 10–13 March 1915.
After a massive artillery barrage, General Sir John French sent the British First Army, under General Haig, against the German-held village of Neuve-Chapelle in French Flanders in an attempt to gain the vital Aubers Ridge. The British took the village but von Falkenhayn rushed 16 000 reserves into the battle and stopped any possibility of a British breakthrough. British casualties, 13 000; German, 14 000. Two other battles were fought in an attempt to capture this ridge; they were as futile and as costly as the first. With their strength in machine-guns the Germans easily held the high ground.

Loos, 25 September–8 October 1915.
The British fought one of the fiercest battles of the war as part of the Allied offensive in Artois, northern France. In this battle the British used poison gas for the first time, though inadvisedly as the wind was blowing in the wrong direction — that is, the gas blew back at the British.

The French attack under General d'Urbal in the Vimy Ridge area and the British attack under General Haig both gained some ground, but von Falkenhayn's counterattack blocked the Allies, though the French struggled on until 14 October. Casualties: German, 178 000; French, 190 000; British, 60 000.

Verdun, 21 February–18 December 1916.
This turned out to be the greatest battles of attrition in history, famous for the heroic French pledge of 'Ils ne passeront pas!'. The vast fortress of Verdun was held by 500 000 men when the German chief-of-staff, von Falkenhayn, organised 1 000 000 men of the Fifth Army, commanded by the Crown Prince Wilhelm himself, for a massive assault. On 21 February 1400 guns bombarded an eight-mile front for twelve hours.

By 23 June — before the Australians had been engaged in a serious battle on the Western Front — the French had suffered 315 000 casualties, the Germans 280 000. Between them the French and Germans fired 40 000 000 shells into the relatively small battlefield and by the time the fighting eased the French had lost 543 000 men and the Germans 434 000.

✦　✦　✦

The battles of 1914–15 established the tactics of the war: Massive frontal attacks by waves of troops supported by drenching artillery fire and many millions of bullets fired by machine-guns. Unfortunately for the French and British, who did most of the attacking after the initial German drives ran out of steam, the defenders also possessed great numbers of troops, and plenty of guns and machine-guns. Throughout the war, the Germans had more machine-guns — the famous Maxim — in action than the Allies could match. Also, the French in particular set up their men as fine targets during the first year of the war: they charged into action clad in a uniform of blue tunics and red trousers.

No nation had prepared for a war of attrition, which meant reciprocal killing and destruction until one side or the other could stand no more. The generals did not know how to fight such a war. The Germans had a natural advantage because their birth rate had increased up to the beginning of the twentieth century, whereas the French birth rate had been declining.

In Britain, Lord Kitchener, the Secretary of State for War — one of those who had agreed that the conflict would soon be over — now announced to everybody's surprise that it would last three or four years and that Great Britain would need to raise an army of 'many millions'. He made this statement at the first cabinet meeting he attended and quite without reference to the Imperial General Staff, most members of which had accompanied the BEF to France.

As the cabinet opposed conscription, Kitchener might have been expected to turn to the eleven divisions of the Territorial Army, but he had an unjustifiably low opinion of the part-time soldiers. Instead, he sought volunteers. He hoped to draw in 100 000 men in the first six months and perhaps 500 000 in all. In fact, a wave of patriotic enthusiasm brought in 500 000 volunteers in the first month and for the next 18 months 100 000 men a month joined the colours. The army was not prepared to receive so many men; it had not enough instructors, camps, uniforms and equipment. Nevertheless, such a deluge of men was to be needed for the killing fields of the Western Front.

It was during the early blood-letting that the trench system of the Western Front came into being. Both sides, unable to make further progress, were desperate to hang on to what they already had. The Germans had one great advantage: the war was not fought on their soil, not then and never during the entire length of the war. While vast areas of France and Belgium were destroyed, with all that this meant in the suffering of refugees and destruction of property, no damage was done to Germany except later in the war when the first bombers in history dropped small bombs on a few enemy targets.

The term Western Front referred to the German western front to distinguish it from their eastern front, against Russia. It was a relatively narrow battlefield 740 kilometres in length, on which, during a period of fifty months, more than 6 000 000 soldiers were killed and another 14 000 000 wounded.

Vast armies confronted one another across belts of barbed wire many miles deep. The wire defended the outer line of trenches that collectively ran for thousands of miles across a morass of mud and, in places, hills and mountains. Fighting raged incessantly for the duration of the war, though some lengths of front were occasionally comparatively quiet. The deaths of 21 000 men and more than 40 000 wounded in one day of battle, as on 1 July 1916, were not cataclysmic enough to bring the madness to an end.

Masses of men could be moved rapidly towards the front because of efficient railway systems, but once the troops were delivered to the railheads their movement was slow, since no army had any mechanical transport and when trucks did come into being they were slow and inadequate in number. For a long time the armies moved no faster than in Napoleon's time, a century earlier.

Defence was largely mechanised, because of the railways, but attack was not. Horses pulled the guns and the transport while the forage for horses occupied more space than ammunition and food.

Australia and the other dominions, Canada, New Zealand, South Africa, Newfoundland and smaller empire territories, had chosen to take part in a war with a terribly high level of bloodshed. Their leaders might not have known that such carnage would ensue but when they found out they still enthusiastically fed their young men into the mincing machine of the Western Front. By 1916 it was clear that Andrew Fisher's pledge of proffering the last Australian man and the last shilling might have to be fulfilled.

CHAPTER 3

The Impotence of Australian Command

The Australian experience at Gallipoli and the AIF's many months in Egypt can have no part in this book, except to say that after the fighting against the Turks on Gallipoli the Australians believed that they could stand up to any conditions, dangers and hardships that might face them in France and Belgium.

The men of the 1st and 2nd Divisions knew little about the war in Europe other than what they occasionally read in the newspapers of Cairo. The ignorance of most of them about what was happening on the Western Front was profound. They were not to know that the battles fought by General Sir John French used up men at a frightening rate. On 25 September 1915, while the Australians were still on Gallipoli, 15 470 men became casualties on the first day of the Battle of Loos. On 11 October a single British division lost 3800 men in ten minutes of fighting. The entire battle cost General French 61 280 casualties — and without gain.

Unknown to the Australians, some British generals considered that they had great soldierly potential. By common British consent, they lacked discipline but they could fight. Early in 1916 the Chief of the Imperial General Staff, in London, telegraphed the British commander in Egypt: 'Three Anzac Divisions in France in April might be worth six at a later date'. He meant that the British and the Canadians were under such pressure that the sooner the Australian divisions arrived the better.

At the end of 1915 General French had been dismissed for his failures and the new British commander-in-chief, General Sir Douglas Haig, had begun planning a major offensive to relieve the German pressure on the French armies.

The newspapers in Cairo emphasised the heroism on the Western Front, and there was plenty of that, rather than the horrors of which there were also many. The heavy casualties were rarely correctly stated and some defeats were presented as victories. The newspaper reports had one important effect — the Australians now knew that the Gallipoli campaign had been a sideshow and they were eager to move on to England, which was 'Home' to most Australians, and then on to the war in France and Belgium.

The transfer came in March 1916, though direct to France, not via England. Lieutenant General Sir William Birdwood, the Briton who had commanded the Australians at Gallipoli, visited each brigade to give them the news, usually during a church parade. He told them that in France they would be among people whose young men were fighting for their country, leaving behind the old men, the women and children. The Australians would be living among these people and serving with British, French and Canadian soldiers, as well as those of France's many colonies. He appealed to the men's honour to uphold the good name of Australia and to justify the reputation they had won at Gallipoli.

The theme of service, honour and probable sacrifice came up in sermons preached by army chaplains on troopships carrying the Australians from Alexandria, Egypt to Marseilles, France. The *Transylvania* had no chaplain so a clergyman turned soldier conducted a service. He was Sergeant, later Lieutenant F. B. Bethune MC and what he told the men demonstrated the moral force which impelled the Australian soldiers.

We know what we have come for, and we know that it is right. We have all read of the things that happened in France. We came of our free wills, to say that this sort of thing shall not happen in the world as long as we are in it. And what if we die? If it were not for the dear ones whom he leaves behind, might not a man pray for a death like that? We know that we are not heroes and we do not wish to be called heroes. Here we are on a great enterprise with no thought of gain or conquest but to help to right a great wrong. With out dear ones behind, and God above and our friends on each side, and only the enemy in front, what more do we wish than that?

When the preacher spoke of 'this sort of thing' he was referring to the atrocities which newspapers alleged the Germans had committed against Belgian and French civilians. In truth, these stories were greatly exaggerated and some were pure fiction. However, false propaganda, ruthlessly used, was a powerful weapon and it had the effect of inciting anger against the enemy in the minds of these modern crusaders from the distant south land and made them want to 'get into the real war'.

On 19 March 1916 troopships carrying the 2nd Division reached Marseilles, where the bands, which had not once been able to play at Gallipoli, struck up the 'La Marseillaise'. The men were wildly excited but the officers retained control, much to the relief of the British staff in the port who had feared riots. Day after day trains carried the Australians through the beautiful countryside of southern France, fresh with spring, into the cold, wet and snowy north. They finished up in billets in barns around St Omer, Aire and Hazebrouck. In the distance the *crump* of shells and the flashes and flares told them that they were indeed approaching 'the real war'.

They were in what the army called the 'Nursery', where reinforcements were trained. The Australians considered themselves veterans and they impatiently endured lectures on many subjects, including how to relieve a trench garrison. On 1 April reconnaissance parties entered the line for the first time, and on the night of 7 April the 2nd Division began to take over a sector. By the middle of that month the two Australian divisions were in the line at Fleurbaix, just south of Armentières. They wore their new steel helmets reluctantly but they welcomed the regular and varied food, the fresh water and life in the villages to which the units were periodically withdrawn for rest.

At this part of the line the Australians did not occupy true trenches. In flat, water-sodden French and Belgian Flanders any excavated trench at once filled with water. The trenches were actually breastworks of mounded earth and sandbags built above ground level and strengthened by anything to hand, such as tree branches, old bedsteads and the wreckage of shelled buildings.

The Australians were better armed than at Gallipoli although their rifles, the 1907 No. 1 Mk III Short Magazine Lee-Enfield, were still the same. Each company of 120 men had one Lewis light machine-gun capable of firing 500 rounds of .303 ammunition per minute. One Lewis per company was a pitifully small allowance; one per section of ten men would have been more appropriate. Every battalion had light, medium and heavy trench mortars, each of which fired bombs at a high trajectory into enemy trenches and behind emplacements. Each division of sixteen battalions had twelve batteries of 18-pounder field-guns, forty-eight guns in all.

The first Australian casualties on the Western Front were two officers and seventy-two men of the 9th Battalion (Queensland) killed or wounded when German shells hit a farmhouse in which they were sheltering three kilometres behind the front. Within days several such farmhouses were shelled and hundreds more Australians became casualties before officers realised that spies were not to blame, as they had instantly supposed. The men had betrayed themselves by hanging out their washing in full view of the enemy or by allowing their open fires to smoke.

The Australians never did fully learn the lesson that carelessness cost lives. Throughout the war men thoughtlessly and sometimes defiantly exposed themselves to view. In some cases it was almost as if they were daring the Germans to shoot. Sometimes it was just too much bother to be careful. Communication trenches were used to get men and materials from the rear to support and front trenches but as they were often muddy and crowded some Australians said, in effect, 'To hell with this! I'm going to walk over the top'. They would climb out of the communication trench and, fully exposed, make their way forward or back to their destination. Most got away with this bravado; many did not.

The Australians' first experience of being the targets of concentrated gunfire occurred on 5 May when the 20th Battalion (NSW) in the Bridoux Salient, came under a two-hour barrage of shells and mortar bombs. More than a hundred men were killed or wounded, and while the experience did not exactly shock the Australians it startled them. Probably for the first time they thought that, after all, trench warfare in France was perhaps worse than at Gallipoli.

On 5 June there was another 'first'. On the south-eastern edge of Armentières the Australians made their first trench raid. Under Captain Maitland Foss, a Western Australian farmer, they rehearsed the raid behind their own lines. A scouting party then cut through the enemy barbed wire and marked a route for the raiders, from the 7th Brigade. Mortar fire was aimed at the point at which the raiders would enter the enemy trench, while artillery created diversions to the south and north before bombarding the target trench directly. The operation was well led and finely timed and the Australians killed some Germans, took prisoners and withdrew.

It had seemed so easy and the Australians soon showed that they had a flair for raiding, but the celerity with which Foss carried out his raid was not normal. Raiding was a dangerous activity. A typical AIF raiding party consisted of six officers and sixty men, divided into two groups, one being responsible for the left of the attack, the other for the right. Each man had a specific duty, as a message-runner, telephone linesman, scout, stretcher-bearer or as a member of a trench party, blocking party, parapet party or intelligence group.

The Australians wore British tunics without any badges so that the enemy would get no information from the body of any Australian killed during the raid. The Australian tunic had capacious blouse pockets with large flaps; the British tunic had slim suitlike pockets with narrower flaps. Hands, faces and bayonet blades were blackened so that they would not reflect moonlight and flares. For mutual recognition in the dark and as an aid for maintaining formation, the men wore white armbands covered with a strip of black cloth which they ripped off as they began their attack. Revolvers instead of rifles were issued to scouts, bombers, carriers and runners. Trench clubs became popular for raiding — short, stout sticks with a lead or iron head. In early raids every man wore black sandshoes for the sake of silent approach, but they proved to be unstable in the mud and slime and were abandoned in favour of regular boots.

During a raid on the night of 25 June 1916 the AIF won its first Victoria Cross in the European theatre of war. Captain K. Heritage led eight officers and seventy-three other ranks, all volunteers from the 5th Brigade, to harass enemy in positions at Bois Grenier, near Armentières. After an artillery barrage which drove the Germans into their deep dugouts, the Australians crossed a ditch under machine-gun fire and broke into the enemy trenches, where engineers blew up two bomb stores. Five minutes later, as the Australians withdrew with prisoners, the Germans attacked with grenades. Thirty Germans were killed in the fight that followed but in No-Man's-Land the Australians came under artillery fire and thirteen were seriously wounded.

Private William Jackson of the 17th Battalion (NSW) escorted a prisoner into the Australian lines and then ran out into a storm of exploding shells to bring in a wounded mate. Having done this he went out again and with a sergeant was bringing in another wounded man when he had his arm practically blown off by a shell. Despite this terrible wound Jackson persisted in his rescue attempt. His arm, hanging only by skin, was amputated in the trench. He was awarded the VC for 'most conspicuous bravery which set an example of pluck and determination'. Only eighteen when he won the VC, Jackson was the youngest of the sixty-five members of the AIF to be so honoured during the Great War.

Losses mounted and in one week at the end of June the Australians had 773 casualties. Such a loss caused concern but the number was less than a 'normal' week's losses for the British Army.

While the 1st and 2nd Divisions were being blooded in the Nursery, the 3rd Division's units were assembled in Australia, and two new divisions, the 4th and 5th, were in Egypt creating their artillery arm. Until the divisions had their complement of gunners they were not really strong enough to go to the Western Front. To man the guns they would be given, each division needed 3000 officers and men, but at that time the 5th had one regular artillery officer and the 4th had none. By inspired leadership and desperately hard work and with the few available guns used in relays, artillery units were formed and trained. British officers who observed the new gunners at practice were surprised at the speed with which Australians could be trained.

The 4th and 5th Divisions relieved the 1st and 2nd in the front line of the Nursery on 5 July, by which time Haig's Somme offensive had been in progress for five days. On 1 July, the day the operation began, the British lost 21 000 men killed and another 40 000 wounded. This was the greatest loss in military history suffered by a single army in one day. A nine-day artillery barrage had preceded the infantry assault but the tremendous weight of shells had neither wiped out nor demoralised the German machine-gunners in their deep concrete shelters.

As the British gunfire eased to allow the infantry to advance, the Germans rushed to the surface with their guns to mow down the British troops, who were stoically advancing at a slow walk, as ordered. They had been told by their generals that they had only 'to stroll over' and occupy the enemy positions. The heavy losses continued but some ground was taken and the British High Command began to replace its tired units with fresh ones from further north, near Lille.

Despite British attempts to conceal the real scale of dead and wounded during the Somme fighting — it was said that many of the wounded British were 'only lightly hurt' — the Australian generals knew of the carnage. They wondered, naturally, what would befall their own units. The Empire armies had no independent existence and the Australian generals were forced to obey orders and commit their divisions to battle on the orders of their British superiors. No Australian officer at this time held a rank higher than major general, and there were few of these. He was distinctly junior to a lieutenant general and a general. This has always confused people not familiar with the army, because majors rank above lieutenants and brigadiers above majors; yet brigadier generals were the lowest rank of general, much inferior to major generals, who were themselves outranked by lieutenant generals.

After the Great War the rank of brigadier general disappeared to be replaced with that of brigadier. In this book, for the sake of simplicity, I refer to brigadiers but it must be remembered that during the war they were brigadier generals.

A brigadier commanded a brigade of four battalions, a major general headed four brigades, which made up a division. A lieutenant general commanded a corps of three divisions while three corps, usually, were an army whose chief was a full general. Many major generals or brigadiers commanded certain large support formations, such as artillery, engineers and supply services.

Being part of a great army was a new experience for Australian senior officers, and nearly all were amateur soldiers. Naturally enough, they were reluctant and hesitant about standing on their relatively junior authority when they were among the many British regular officers of their own rank and above. Their own chief was a British regular, Lieutenant General Sir William Birdwood, who had commanded the Anzacs at Gallipoli. Mostly it was Birdwood who spoke for the AIF in the conferences of the British High Command. In the British Army rank structure it was virtually impossible in 1916 and 1917 for the Australian senior officers to have their viewpoint listened to, much less acted upon. Had they been able to follow their own convictions it is very likely that certain operational planning would have been amended.

On a few occasions Australian divisional and brigade commanders demurred when confronted with an operational plan which seemed to them flawed and unacceptably dangerous, but in the end they were compelled to do what they were ordered to do.

The Australians' first major battle on the Western Front, at Fromelles, 19–20 July 1916, was a disaster and it profoundly affected the attitude of the AIF for the rest of the war. It had the direct effect of bringing about the longing of all the Australians to be under their own commanders. The leaders themselves were frustrated and exasperated that they were unable to plan some operations by themselves. They realised that strategy had to be decided at a political and higher military level, but they would liked to have been consulted about tactics.

Not being officers of a regular army, and coming from civilian life in which they were successful with their careers, senior Australian officers were accustomed to being listened to. It was galling for them to find in France and Belgium that they were little more than administrators for their respective divisions and brigades. John Monash, with his vision and imagination as well as his disciplined and trained mind, must have been acutely aware of his limitations of action outside his division, the 3rd.

While this book mainly concerns the Battle of Hamel rather than that of Fromelles, it is necessary to describe Fromelles in some detail in order to make clear the 'political' helplessness of the Australian military leaders on the Western Front in mid-1916 compared with their significantly greater authority in mid-1918.

CHAPTER 4

Fromelles: How to Lose a Battle

The Battle of Fromelles in July 1916 was the result of the reverses the British were suffering in the Battle of the Somme. The flawed manner of the handling of the Fromelles battle was the result of the deficiencies in the British officer corps of the period. The general responsible for the Fromelles operation was Lieutenant General Sir Richard Haking, who had taken a brigade to France in 1914 as part of the BEF. In that era, officer ranks of the army worked on the protector-protégé system. Every officer on his way up needed a man more senior to bring him along; in return, the junior could be expected to back his mentor to the hilt. Haking, only a year younger than General Sir Douglas Haig, was Haig's protégé and he gave his allegiance to Haig when he commanded British First Army in France 1914–15, rather than to General Sir John French, the BEF commander-in-chief.

As an infantryman, Haking should have had a natural 'feel' for the trench-warfare conditions that were developing at the end of 1914. But it must be understood that infantry officers of the period, at least the battalion commander, his adjutant and the company commanders, rode horses and rarely had to march. Few officers of any rank carried packs and kitbags; these weighty encumbrances were managed by the officer's batman — generally called his 'servant' in the British Army. Much of their baggage came up with the unit transport and it included many creature comforts, such as camp beds. Officers could afford to send home for good quality boots and trench-waders; some even had their own mincing machines in order to make army-issue meat more palatable and 'hampers from Harrods' were commonplace. In addition, officers were not burdened with the 9½ pound (4.3 kilogram) weight of the SMLE rifle and bayonet; their personal weapon was the much lighter .455 Webley revolver.

Few divisional commanders had the remotest idea of the hideous difficulty in attacking across muddy ground against an enemy firing machine-guns from behind defences of barbed wire and sandbagged emplacements. Haking gave this problem no thought and his battle plans made no allowance for the state of the ground, the weather or the condition of the soldiers themselves.

At Staff College, the self-opinionated Haking, with a professional status as a teacher of strategy and tactics, had not merely ridiculed the defensive, he exalted the attack. This may have been sound as a principle but Haking took it even further — he claimed that the attack would succeed even if the stronger force was on the defensive and the weaker on the offensive. This was patently nonsense. 'The offensive will win as sure as there is a sun in the heavens,' he said.

For this general, then commanding a division and soon to command a corps, the modern battlefield was 'simply' a matter of morale and human nature. As he saw it, men naturally favoured defence and never the attack; this weakness had to be reversed by the men's mastering their own 'human nature'. Haking was worried that British and Empire troops would be deficient in aggressive spirit so he constantly preached the offensive to this officers and men.

Observing the Germans' use of massive firepower, Haking came up with the answer to it — the offensive. 'One often hears it stated,' he said, 'that with modern weapons the defence has gained over the attack. If, however, it was possible to visit the front line of attack and talk to the officers, NCOs and men, and then go over to the defenders' trenches and talk to them, one would discover why the attack is better than the defence'.

The reasons he adduced for this conclusion are keenly relevant to his handling of the Australian troops under his command at Fromelles and the way in which all the senior British generals handled their men for most of the war. *It was all to do with morale.* Haking's image of war, just prior to the conflict of 1914, was that of an orderly battlefield in which British soldiers would be controlled by imposed discipline and self-discipline. In this he was echoing a War Office manual of 1909, *Training and Manoeuvre Regulations*, which stated, 'Moral force in modern war predominates over physical force as greatly as formerly'.

Haking and others spoke of a 'psychological battlefield'. He quoted ad nauseam Napoleon's maxim that in war the moral predominated over the physical in a ratio of three to one. He seems not to have understood that in Napoleon's day the machine-gun was unknown, nor were high-explosive shells. Haking even advocated tight infantry formations in the attack, shoulder-to-shoulder style, since in this way the troops could, he said, 'take strength and comfort from each other'.

A century before he disseminated this advice, infantry stood shoulder-to-shoulder, often in three ranks narrowly separated, as a defence against attack by cavalry. The disciplined firepower of a line of men standing or kneeling side by side was devastating against horseman, as it had been in the case of the Argyll and Sutherland Highlanders — 'the thin red line' — at Balaclava in 1855.

In Continental warfare of the period, when muskets were muzzle-loaded and fired a single ball, cannons smashed gaps in the close-set infantry ranks but did not wipe them out. The advent of quickfire rifles and exploding shells changed all that. Yet here was Haking urging shoulder-to-shoulder advances while enemy machine-guns sprayed destructive sheets of lead bullets across the battlefield!

Soldiers who were ordered to go forward shoulder-to-shoulder were killed in this formation. More or less in this manner, tens of thousands of British soldiers had already been mown down at First Ypres, at Loos, Neuve Chapelle and on other killing fields. French troops, nourished for decades in the tactics of la gloire — glory charges — had also been savaged in this way by German machine-guns.

During the first days of the Battle of the Somme there had occurred one of the most ghastly debacles in history when British troops were sent across open slaughter fields in the old, steady, brave British way.

Haking sent a document to Haig's GHQ proposing two separate operations. The smaller attack would cut off Boar's Head Salient near Aubers. The larger action would be a full-scale battle below the Aubers Ridge village of Fromelles. Conforming to Haking's plan, the 116th Brigade of the 39th (British) Division delivered the attack on 29 June. It was a total failure with heavy loss. Haking sacked the divisional general for the reverse, though in the GHQ communiqué the attack appeared as 'a successful raid'. This upgrading of a disaster was an example of Haig's protecting his protégé Haking.

General Sir Herbert Plumer, GOC Second Army, and General Sir Charles Monro, GOC First Army, had discussed Haking's idea to carry out the larger operation at the junction of the two armies. Following the catastrophic British losses during the first few weeks of the Somme battle, Haking's suggestion now seemed more attractive when Plumer and Monro were told that the Germans had withdrawn probably nine divisions from the Lille sector to strengthen even further their Somme front.

Haig 'desired' Haking's operation — variously referred to as Aubers, Fromelles and Fleurbaix — to be put into effect. It was to be a 'purely local' attack intended to hold the Germans to their ground and prevent their reinforcing their Somme line. That day Haking received orders from Monro that the preliminary bombardment should give the impression of an 'offensive operation on large scale'. The infantry objective would be limited to the German front line system. The details were left to Haking, who planned to use the British 61st Division and the Australian 5th Division, which was commanded by Major General James Whiteside McCay.

The conditions under which the attack would have to be made were obvious at the time and hindsight has no relevance to the account of this battle. Haking was committing his troops to an advance on a front of three-and-a-half kilometres across the flat waterlogged French Flanders farmland under the eyes of the many German observers on Aubers Ridge, less than a mile away. During daylight hours — which amounted to eighteen hours in midsummer — they watched all the British operations for the attack. During the previous fourteen months the Germans had steadily strengthened their breastwork defences, which included hundreds of machine-gun emplacements built of concrete, well sited and camouflaged. The machine-gunners and the artillerymen further behind them knew to a yard the range to every tactical point on the battlefield. They had set ranging markers in No-Man's-Land and they even had nightlamps, visible one-way only, to help their aim at night.

For the attackers everything depended on the destructiveness of the British artillery and the speed of the infantry advance, but the nearer the soldiers approached, the closer would be enemy observation and the stronger the opposition.

Any digging by the twelve Australian and British battalions involved would soon reach water level, and therefore they would have to build up sandbag breastworks, a laborious and time-consuming task that left the men vulnerable. Holding any ground gained would be difficult.

The scheme of operations was almost identical to that of Haking's Battle of Aubers Ridge in May 1915 and the opposing enemy defenders were the same good soldiers of the 6th Bavarian Reserve Division of four regiments. Haking told his divisional commanders that 'the narrow width of the attack should make it possible, with the ammunition available, to reduce the defenders to a state of collapse before the assault'. This was absurd. He had been on the Western Front since 1914, nowhere had he seen the German defenders reduced to 'a state of collapse' and he was aware that a massive nine-day bombardment before the Somme offensive of 1 July had not done so. Yet at Fromelles he was anticipating such a result in three days on a front where he himself had been defeated in May 1915 and June 1916.

Because of bad weather General Monro proposed to cancel the operation but Haig overruled him, possibly to show his belief that a thrusting attack could still succeed.

Two days before the battle a worried Australian senior officer demurred. This courageous officer was Brigadier Brudenell White, chief-of-staff to General Sir William Birdwood, GOC 1 Anzac Corps. White had one of the finest analytical organisational brains of the war. He was perceptive and he thought every action through to what was to him its logical conclusion. He stated that he hoped the operation would be postponed indefinitely. The British staff, he said, was underestimating the Germans' intelligence if they supposed that they would take a British attack seriously when they knew that it had no reserves behind it. And this they must know from their own observation, reconnaissance, patrols, overflights by spotter aircraft and information from spies.

White's intervention — which must have been sanctioned by his chief, Birdwood — was an unprecedented 'liberty', a breach of military etiquette by an officer who was relatively junior in British Army terms. That he was a senior officer in the AIF gave him no additional authority in British Army circles.

This was the first recorded instance of an Australian officer daring to criticise a British general's staff, indeed that of the commander-in-chief himself.

It was further suggested to Haking that he could achieve the desired result of holding the Germans in position north of the Somme by making a powerful demonstration, with many guns and many units openly arriving and apparently establishing themselves as if preparing for a big offensive. Haking did not think in such a shrewd way. Despite the trail of blood already spilled by his own soldiers, victory was just a matter of a vigorous attack culminating in a bayonet charge. The battle that ensued was a predictable shambles in the true meaning of that word — a slaughter.

The assault was to go in at 6 pm on 19 July. At that time of the year the sun would be shining until 9 pm and darkness would not fall until 10 pm, so the attackers would be going forward on an open plain on which there was no cover and without darkness or gloom to hide their movements. The artillery barrage, not just sporadic shelling but sustained and systematic gunfire for three days, warned the Germans that an attack was imminent. Also, from their higher ground they saw increased movement of transport, guns and men in the British–Australian lines.

They shelled the AIF 8th Brigade, tensely waiting in their trenches, before they went over the top. No-Man's-Land was 150 to 250 metres wide and German machine-gun fire was heavy from the start. Despite casualties, the Australians of the 8th, 14th and 15th Brigades cleared the Germans from their front trenches, and following waves of infantry captured the support trenches. This was quite an achievement and in a short time the exultant Diggers were in open country beyond the German positions, though they in no way threatened the enemy hold on the ridge, which was still far ahead of them. This was the only important fight on the Western Front when the Germans did not face Australians wearing steel helmets. Having yet to be issued with the 'tin hats' which the British command had insisted they wear, they were distinctively decked out in their familiar slouch hats.

The Australians' objective was a third trench line, but they could not find it. In fact, it did not exist; the British staff had made a mistake. After sheltering from enemy fire in a mire of ditches and shell-holes, the Australians made a rough line of their own by joining up the ditches and using sandbags filled with mud. Three hours later, as a blessed darkness fell, the battalions established some kind of order.

The 8th and 14th Brigades had captured more than 1000 metres of trench, a considerable achievement, but the 14th Brigade's flank was dangerously exposed. Haking ordered the British 61st Division to attack at 9 pm to reduce the pressure on the 14th Brigade. The depleted 15th Brigade also attacked, only to discover, far too late, that the 61st attack had been cancelled. Nevertheless, during a night of fierce fighting, the 15th extended the front held by the 14th.

As a precaution, the Germans rushed support battalions into the line, but the only reinforcements available to the Australians were the carrying parties. Having taken up supplies, they stayed to fight. In night-long hand-to-hand fighting and bombing, the Germans worked their way around the flanks of the Australians. Before 6 pm on 20 July the 8th Brigade's position was critical. Forced out of their trenches and vulnerable in the open, the men turned around and charged through the Germans, who were now spread across No-Man's-Land, in a desperate attempt to get back to their own original position. The 14th Brigade was now hopelessly isolated and at 8 o'clock next morning the exhausted men were ordered to pull out. Many did so through a shallow communications trench that had been dug during the night.

Many prodigious acts of valour were performed as isolated parties held out under young officers demonstrating exemplary leadership. Many men fell, never to be seen again, while some surrendered rather than face pointless slaughter. As the battle ended on the evening of 20 July the front-line trenches were filled with casualties while the regimental medical officers worked feverishly to cope with the flow of wounded. C. E. W. Bean recorded that after the battle ended, 'in front of the 15th Brigade the wounded would be seen everywhere raising their limbs in pain or turning hopelessly, hour after hour, from one side to the other'.

For a time there was an unofficial truce but it ended on the orders of Major General McCay, himself following instructions from the British Command. Nevertheless, for another three days and nights, small groups of Australians, sometimes one man, brought in wounded. When the truce ended the Germans neither rescued suffering men, whom they could have reached, nor did they allow the Australians to do so, but some tried.

The Battle of Fromelles was known to many Australians at the time as the Battle of Fleurbaix, the name of a town nearby where the battalions formed up for the operation. It was a military disaster but it was a victory for the Australian spirit. The 5th Division lost 5533 officers and men in twenty-seven hours of battle. The 60th Battalion (Victoria) went into the fight 887 strong; after the battle only one officer and 106 men answered roll call. The 32nd Battalion (Western Australia/South Australia) had seventeen officers and 701 men hit; the 59th (Victoria) twenty officers and 675 men. Four hundred Australians were taken prisoner, a record number for the Great War.

These appalling losses shocked their own senior officers, some of whom were deeply angry at what they considered inept military leadership. The most vocal and forthright was Brigadier H. E. 'Pompey' Elliott, commander of the 15th Brigade. But such casualties were 'normal' at the time. The British, after nearly two years of attritional war, were accustomed to them. Many Australians, including journalists, stated that such losses must not happen again. They blamed Major General McCay for the debacle but he was as much a victim of the High Command's planning as any of his soldiers.

Before the battle, Brigadier Elliott had condemned the operation as 'insane'. When it was over he said: 'The whole operation from beginning to end was so incredibly blundered that it is almost incomprehensible how those who were responsible for it could have consisted of trained professional soldiers of considerable reputation and experience and why, in the outcome of this extraordinary adventure, any of them was retained in active command'.

General Haking defended his leadership by claiming that Fromelles failed solely because the infantry were new to battle. While this may have been a factor, the operation failed for six main reasons:

- the planning was lamentably poor;
- the military objective was not a standard target requiring regular methods of attack; it was nothing more than water-filled abandoned trenches and ditches;
- the front was too narrow and the Germans could therefore defend it in depth and rapidly reinforce it;
- the enemy artillery had not been knocked out; German observers on the ridge directed their guns onto the targets and the British planners must have known they would do this;

- the British guns failed to destroy the German machine-gun posts; certainly these were well-concealed but they were in obvious places, behind logs for instance, which should have been pulverised; and
- while the 5th Division was going forward, the British 61st Division was in its original position; had these troops captured the German salient known as the Sugar Loaf, poking deeply into No-Man's-Land, the Germans could not have fired on the Australians from the rear, with disastrous effect.

There is yet another point and one that was not lost on the Australian senior officers. The stated purpose for the attack was to prevent the German High Command from moving divisions based near Lille south to the Somme. It had earlier been pointed out by Brigadier White and others that this could more easily have been achieved by a large British–Australian build-up in the Aubers Ridge sector to convince the Germans that a major assault was imminent, leading them to hold all their divisions in the north. Such a threat, provided the deception was believed, could have been even more effective than an actual assault.

Once the smaller attack had expended itself — as it was bound to do — the German High Command could do whatever it wished. In the event it destroyed the British–Australian advance *and* moved its divisions south. For the Germans, Fromelles was a double victory.

Lieutenant General Haking reported to Haig: 'The Australian infantry attacked in a most gallant manner and gained the enemy's position but they were not sufficiently trained to consolidate the ground gained. The attack, though it failed, has done both divisions a great deal of good'.

It was true that the 5th Division was not fully trained, but not even thoroughly trained and experienced troops could have consolidated territory won at Fromelles. Suppose they had been able to dig deep trenches and protect them with sandbags, the Germans with their overwhelming firepower and the advantage of higher ground could have quickly demolished them. Any ground won at Fromelles was a death trap.

Despite the horrendous losses, I repeat, Haking claimed that the defeat had 'done both divisions a great deal of good'. This statement was spurious. In truth, the operation had in no way been a benefit for the British division. As for doing the AIF 5th Division 'a great deal of good', the attack had crippled it. The traumatic shock of Fromelles, coupled with the staggering casualties, might have finished many a division as a fighting force. It said much for the resilience of the AIF and the quality of its infantry that before the end of summer 1916 the 5th Division recovered. Its battalions, reinforced and brought back to strength, were again vigorously raiding German trenches.

Haking's attack at Fromelles was damned by Captain Philip Landon, on the staff of the 182nd Infantry Brigade, and he also criticised Haig's role in it. 'The weakness of GHQ lay in not seeing that a Corps commander, left to himself, would be tempted to win glory for his Corps by a spectacular success and would be prodigal in using the divisions that passed through his hands.'

Despite the Fromelles debacle, Haig did not abandon Haking and send him home. Far from it — in August he attempted to appoint his protégé, thruster and proven failure as GOC First Army. In London, the Imperial General Staff was appalled. The Deputy Chief of the General Staff, Lieutenant General Sir Henry Wilson, wrote: 'It [the suggestion that Haking be promoted] shows how hopelessly out of touch GHQ is with what we think of Haking'. General Sir William Robertson, Chief of the Imperial General Staff, agreed with Wilson and prevented the promotion. The way Haig manoeuvred men into senior positions, and the choice of his appointments, were causing such concern that George V himself, usually Haig's protector, told him that senior appointments should be made in London, not at GHQ in France. Haig's most ardent apologists would find it difficult to defend him over his decision to promote Haking, who was always 'Butcher Haking' after Fromelles.

The disaster which had befallen the 5th Division at Fromelles cracked the foundations of the trust that the Australians from major generals down to private soldiers had in British senior leadership. Further calamities utterly destroyed that trust. The difference between Haking's conduct at Fromelles and that of Monash at Le Hamel, almost exactly two years later, is immense. Haking's performance was pitiful; that of Monash was masterly.

The further calamities to which I have already referred need to be outlined in order to understand the evolution of Australian military thinking and the impetus which drove it to full maturity at Hamel.

Were a military disaster on the scale of Fromelles to occur to Australian soldiers towards the end of the twentieth century it would quickly erupt into a political storm with bitter recriminations directed against the British authorities. The presence of the media in all its strength — television, radio and print, with blanket coverage and instant transmission — would have been a force in itself. Within a day, everybody in Australia would have known what had happened. At the time of Fromelles in 1916, defaulting generals were protected not only by stringent censorship but by the lapse in time between the disaster and awareness of it in Australia. In 1916 there was no way in which the leaders in Australia could fully know what had happened. The public knew nothing whatever.

CHAPTER 5

Gaining Fame, Losing Men

In July and August 1916 the 1st, 2nd and 4th Divisions took part in battles which, by General Haking's measuring stick, would do them 'a great deal of good'. At Pozières they suffered more than 23 000 casualties in six weeks.

The Battle of the Somme had been raging for twenty-three days when the AIF 1st Division was introduced to it. Pozières was situated on a long gradually rising ridge and covered the approaches to Thiepval, a higher point to the north. If the British could capture Pozières they could outflank Thiepval. To prevent this, the Germans had made Pozières immensely strong. From their trenches and machine-gun posts they had a clear, gently graded field of fire over all possible lines of enemy advance.

Between 13 and 17 July British infantry had bravely made four attacks against the warren of trenches. Their final charge was made after a bombardment so heavy that it reduced the already battered village to rubble, but the Germans held firm and practically nothing was gained on the ridge — for a cost of 12 000 casualties.

However, the High Command was left with one advantage. South of Pozières the British attack had pushed further forward than the Pozières line, which meant that in a fresh assault the British could attack the Germans not only from the west but also from the south. The 1st Division was to make this attack on 23 July.

The Australians took some ground and performed heroically but the Germans, fearing a break in their line, kept up a three-day artillery barrage. Charles Bean commented that the Australians went through the barrages 'as you would go through a summer shower — too proud to bend their heads, many of them, because their mates were looking'.

In three days the 1st Division lost 5285 officers and men, the rest were exhausted and the division was replaced by the 2nd Division. Sergeant

E. J. Rule, 14th Battalion, who saw the men of the 1st Division move into a rest area, wrote that they 'looked like men who had been in hell, drawn and haggard and so dazed that they appeared to be walking in a dream and their eyes looked glassy and starey'.

The 2nd Division had an equally bloody introduction to major battle on the Western Front. Lieutenant J. A. Raws of the 23rd Battalion (Victoria), a journalist in civil life, wrote graphically about the night of 31 July:

We lay down terror-stricken along a bank. The shelling was awful ... We had to drive the men [to dig] by every possible means and dig ourselves. The wounded and killed had to be thrown to one side. I refused to let any sound man help a wounded man. The sound men had to dig. We dug on and finished amid a tornado of bursting shells. I was buried twice and thrown down several times — buried with dead and dying. The horror was indescribable.

Raws, who saw officers go mad from the strain, was himself killed at Pozières three weeks later.

Haig's judgment was that the 2nd Division's attack had failed because of lack of planning. Visiting the AIF office at Contay, Somme, he told Birdwood and Brudenell White, 'You're not fighting Bashi-Bazouks now'. This was a patronising reference to Haig's unwarranted low opinion of Turks as fighters. Birdwood and White, having spent nine months at Gallipoli, knew how formidable the Turks were. White was proud of his men and ever ready to defend them. Resenting Haig's supercilious attitude, he told him that while mistakes had been made at Pozières, the commander-in-chief was wrong in his opinions about the Australians' preparations for battle.

Haig's staff indicated to White by headshakes and frowns that a brigadier should not be so presumptuous in speaking to his chief. White, from the fortress of his brilliant mind, pressed on. He explained that the C-in-C's assumptions were based on incorrect information and then, point by point, he explained exactly what had happened. He was polite but persistent and the senior officers present, including Birdwood, expected Haig to reprimand White or freeze him out of the discussion. In a way he did this, by putting his hand on White's shoulder and saying, 'I dare say you are right, young man'. As White was in his forties, this too was patronising. It appears that Birdwood did not openly support his chief-of-staff during this exchange.

The 2nd Division fought so well that Haig, acting on reports from General Sir Hubert Gough, commanding the Reserve Army of which the Australian divisions were part, telegraphed that the Australian success was of 'very considerable importance and opens the way to further equally valuable successes'.

But by the time the 2nd Division handed over its lines to the AIF 4th Division, at dusk on 4 August, it had lost 6848 officers and men. These shocking losses, coming on top of those inflicted upon the 1st and 5th Divisions, strained the ability of AIF Headquarters staff to find reinforcements fresh from Australia. Soldiers finishing their convalescence after wounds and illness, and other men weeded out of base units, were used to make up the numbers required. Some individual unit losses give a clear view of the problem. The 4th Pioneer Battalion lost eight officers and 222 men in keeping open one length of trench. The 27th Battalion had 100 men left out of a nominal 800; the 28th Battalion, 130 men.

The 4th Division was depleted and exhausted after losing 7100 men and was withdrawn to be replaced by the 1st Division, still a third under strength from its earlier mauling. It lost a further ninety-two officers and 2558 men in its strenuous efforts to capture the fortified Mouquet Farm. Now the 2nd Division was brought back from its rest. In its four days in the line it lost 1268 more men. It was considered spent and the 4th Division came back for a second blooding. Its 13th Brigade lost forty-one officers and 1305 men.

The AIF was used as a battering ram seven times on Pozières Ridge. The 1st Division's casualties were 7000, the 2nd's 8100, the 4th's 7100. This was 50 per cent of their original fighting strength. Of the overall total fewer than 200 were prisoners, and of these more than half were wounded when captured. The Canadians took over from the AIF, which was withdrawn and sent to the Ypres Salient in Flanders. They were considered to have earned a rest in a sector of relative quiet, but worse ordeals than Pozières awaited them.

They were back on the Somme for a campaign in the winter of 1916–17 — the coldest for a century, according to the French. For Australians, accustomed to mild winters, the conditions were appalling. Fighting went on in deep, syrupy mud, in falling snow and driving rain. Spring came and a general movement forward took place as the Germans steadily pulled back to stronger positions. Tactically they were better off because they now had a shorter front. The British armies had suffered about 650 000 casualties since 1 July.

When the Germans withdrew to their Hindenburg Line the Australian leaders in the field were given further unfortunate proof that their own generals needed more control over the actions to which the Diggers were committed. The Hindenburg Line was a formidable defence system, including three wide swathes of barbed wire in front of their front-line trenches. In numerous places the Germans shrewdly placed the wire in triangular patterns so that their machine-guns could fire along their edges. They also expected that the triangle points, where lengths of wire met, would split the waves of attacking troops. The always methodical Germans had placed aiming marks in No-Man's-Land so that there would be no hit-and-miss gunfire. The Hindenburg Line incorporated many tunnels, concrete bunkers and gun emplacements.

The infantry attackers would come from the AIF 4th Division, commanded now by Major General W. Holmes. On 9 April 1917 a British junior officer of tanks, Major W. H. L. Watson, reported to Gough's HQ that his twelve machines could break down the German wire on the Bullecourt front, thus opening the way for the infantry. Perhaps Watson was very persuasive in his presentation, perhaps Gough was so desperate for a victory that he was prepared to try the tanks. General Birdwood and Brigadier White disliked the idea because tanks had yet to be proven. Sweeping aside their objections, Gough ordered Holmes to attack German positions east of Bullecourt on 10 April.

This gave little time for preparation and Holmes considered Gough's plan foolhardy, but his objections were ignored. He ordered the 4th Brigade (Brigadier C. H. Brand) and 12th Brigade (Brigadier J. C. Robertson) to get ready for immediate attack. Just before midnight Birdwood, back at 1 Anzac Corps HQ, read reconnaissance patrol reports that bombardment had made no apparent impact on the German wire, that the enemy was alert and that the front trenches were fully manned. Urgently, Birdwood telephoned Gough to say the attack was risky. He was coldly informed that General Haig himself wanted the attack to go forward. Following a later message that a British attack at Arras had suffered a serious setback, Brudenell White also protested about the Bullecourt plan. Gough responded that the Arras reverse made his operation all the more urgent.

The Diggers, lying sleepless in fresh snow, eagerly waited for the British tanks which they had been told would make life so much easier for infantry. Held up by bad weather, the tanks did not arrive and the Australians were pulled out in haste before the Germans saw them. A supporting British division, unaware of the change of plan, did attack Bullecourt and lost heavily.

Having lost confidence in the tanks, Birdwood and White again tried to have the plan cancelled. Gough referred their objections to Haig, who rejected them and ordered the attack to begin at 4.30 am on 11 April.

The 4th Division had leaders resolute, courageous and skilled enough to make the ambitious assault succeed, but the tanks were quickly knocked out or stalled in the mud. A tank mistook the 4th Brigade for Germans and fired into one of their trenches. Remarkably, considering the enemy resistance, some companies fought their way into German trenches. Brigadiers Brand and Robertson called for artillery fire to support their men but the British 5th Army artillery commander, Lieutenant Colonel R. L. R. Rabett, refused to fire. His own observers had told him, mistakenly, that British tanks and Australian troops were well beyond the Hindenburg Line; shells from his guns there would destroy them.

Brand and Robertson insisted that those reports were wrong and urged Rabett to open fire. When he still refused, the Australian brigadiers hurriedly contacted Birdwood, who felt compelled to back the artillery commander. Thus the Australian infantry was left unprotected by British artillery. Vainly, the forward Australians sent up flare signals asking for shells to be dropped onto the German gun positions firing at them.

The situation became so desperate that there was no option but to retire. The firing stopped about 2 pm, nearly ten hours after it had begun. The 4th Brigade had sent 3000 officers and men into the battle; their casualties amounted to 2339. The 12th Brigade suffered 950 casualties from the 2000 men engaged. Of the overall casualty total, twenty-eight officers and 1142 men were captured, by far the largest number of Australians taken prisoner in a single battle during the war.

Many of the prisoners had been wounded.

Withdrawn from the Bullecourt front, the 4th Division survivors were marched back to rest huts in the Albert area. Birdwood sent them a message: 'We have no cause to be disheartened at having failed to maintain our footing. Rather we can be proud of the magnificent bravery displayed'. A week later Birdwood, with Brigadier Brand, visited the 4th Division's camp to tell the survivors about their vain efforts to have Gough's battle tactics for Bullecourt changed. Lieutenant E. J. Rule wrote in his diary that the generals had 'tears in their eyes'.

The Australian generals had not been insistent enough with Gough. Birdwood, so strongly against Gough's decision to attack, and then against his plans, could have gone direct to Haig or his chief-of-staff.

Second Bullecourt was fought on practically the same ground as the first battle, between 3 and 17 May. The role of the AIF 2nd Division was to attack the German positions known as OG 1 and OG 2 lines and capture some fortified villages well beyond them, with the British 62nd Division attacking alongside. With the experience of First Bullecourt to guide them, Major General N. M. Smyth and his brigadiers prepared, they believed, for all possible emergencies. The stunt was rehearsed behind the lines and, by the time the battle began, the division and brigade staffs had done a good professional job. It was an epic battle and on 6 May General Haig was impressed enough to comment: 'The capture of the Hindenburg Line east of Bullecourt, and the manner in which it was held against such constant and desperate attempts to retake it will rank high among the great deeds of the war and help appreciably in wearing the enemy out. The fine initiative shown by all commanders down to the lowest is admirable'.

But the Australians were also 'wearing out'. The 1st Division and then the 5th became involved. The fighting finished on 17 May because both sides were exhausted. Second Bullecourt was an achievement and the failure of one of the AIF brigades did not diminish that achievement but enhanced it. The 2nd Division held the territory it had taken and the captured German lines remained part of the British front line until March 1918, when a great German spring offensive swept aside almost the entire British line. To a large extent the victor of Second Bullecourt was Brigadier John Gellibrand. He had so inspired his officers with his own professionalism that they had made the 6th Brigade into probably the finest brigade of the AIF at that time. Nevertheless, another 7000 Diggers had become casualties.

At Messines in June 1917 the AIF 3rd Division, under John Monash, together with elements of the 4th Division and the entire New Zealand Division, won what was considered the greatest Allied victory of the war to that time, though the AIF suffered 6800 casualties. Monash's insistence on detailed planning was noticeable at Messines and on this occasion his British chief, General Sir Herbert Plumer, GOC Second Army, was equally dedicated to detailed preparations.

The battles of the Ypres Salient which followed Messines — Menin Road and Polygon Wood among them — were victories for the AIF, but, as always, costly ones. The Battle of Broodseinde Ridge in October was the most expensive in lives. In a quagmire, under driving rain and incessant enemy fire, the AIF divisions made progress as the spearhead of what was more generally known as the Battle of Passchendaele, but they suffered 38 000 casualties in eight weeks. This was the AIF's share of 448 614 British and Empire casualties since 31 July 1917.

It was predicted that the AIF could survive only by feeding upon itself. The service troops from transport and all other rear-echelon units would have to become infantry, machine-gunners and artillerymen. The training units would be broken up and perhaps some front-line battalions would be disbanded to supply reinforcements to other battalions. According to pessimists, the AIF was unlikely to remain an élite.

However, it did retain its reputation, even though its men knew that with each battle their own chances of survival were slim. Captain R. J. Henderson of the 13th Battalion expressed the feelings of many Diggers when he wrote in April 1918: 'A few years of this and one treats life very cheaply. Lately some of our officers have been killed who landed with the battalion on 25 April [at Gallipoli], so that apparently it is only a matter of time. One must look at this game from a philosophic standpoint'.

That standpoint was fatalism, according to Lieutenant A. W. Mann of the 25th Battalion, who wrote home during the same period: 'You can't stop a shell from bursting in your trench. You can't stop the rain or prevent a light [flare] going up just as you are halfway over the parapet.

So what on earth is the use of worrying? So smile, damn you, smile'.

Militarily, the AIF had something to smile about when they fought two successful battles at Villers-Bretonneux in 1918, the first between 30 March and 12 April and the second, 23–27 April. British and French commanders were generous in their praise for the Australian counterattack at Villers-Bretonneux. Brigadier Grogan VC, who saw the action by night across unknown and difficult ground, regarded it as 'perhaps the greatest individual feat of the war'.

Several officers claimed credit for the Villers-Bretonneux success, including General Haig, General Rawlinson, commanding the British Fourth Army, and General Butler, commanding III Corps. The officer who pressed his claims least of all, Brigadier T. W. Glasgow of AIF 13th Brigade, deserved the greatest praise. Courageously, he disputed the plan which his British superior, General Heneker, wanted to press upon the Australians. The incident is historically important because it happened only two months before Hamel and it showed Australian brigadiers were at long last prepared to assert themselves. Glasgow saw the dangerous implications of Heneker's plan and politely but firmly said, 'Sir, it's against all the teaching of your own army to attack across the enemy's front. My troops would get hell from the enemy's right'.

Heneker resented Glasgow's display of independence. The atmosphere became strained and Heneker several times referred by telephone to the corps commander, Butler. Glasgow went on stressing that he would do what was asked of him, but with his own tactics. And, he said, he would start at 10.30 pm, not Heneker's 8 pm. Glasgow knew that at the earlier time the light would still be too bright and his men would be easily visible. Angry, Heneker again called the corps commander. Putting down the telephone, he said to Glasgow, 'General Butler wants the job done at 8 pm'.

Glasgow exploded. 'If it was God Almighty who gave the order we couldn't do it in daylight! Your artillery is largely out of action and the enemy is in position with all his guns.' Again the matter was referred to Butler and Glasgow was asked successively whether 8.30, 9 or 9.30 pm would suit him. Finally he conceded half an hour and said that he would start at 10 pm. It was still too early and when the 13th Brigade assembled it was observed and fired upon.

Like Glasgow, Brigadier Elliott of the 15th Brigade had the better of his own interview with Heneker. He had already given his orders and he amended them only when Glasgow, meeting him at 8 pm, suggested improvements. The brigadiers' attack was eminently successful.

During 1916 and 1917 Australian brigadiers could not have taken such a stubborn stand against foolish orders from their British superiors. The episode in April 1918 marked a turning point in Australian command maturity.

With renewed confidence, the Australian infantry embarked on a period which became known as 'peaceful penetration'. This was a fine euphemism for capturing and killing Germans quietly and without loss to the Australian patrols involved. Seldom more than a platoon in strength and generally led by a lieutenant, sergeant or corporal, the Diggers made numerous silent raids on the Somme and Lys Sector, away to the north, during the period April–June 1918. Monash's 3rd Division was particularly successful, taking prisoners on three days out of every five. In the 41st Battalion, the capturing of Germans developed into an unofficial company competition, with B Company the winner. In one exploit Lieutenant R. Tredenick's patrol rushed a post, killing nine enemy and dragging back two survivors, without loss to themselves. Having any of your own men killed or wounded during peaceful penetration was considered unprofessional.

One of the finest exploits took place near Hamel on 5 April. Corporal D. A. Sayers of the 58th Battalion, leading only a few men, cut off and captured a German officer and thirty men. Lieutenant A. W. Irvine, intelligence officer of the 17th Battalion, made an opportunist raid with twenty Diggers on a German trench near Morlancourt. First two sleepy sentries were captured at bayonet point; a single grenade killed four enemy in a dugout and another twenty-two surrendered. From the moment Irvine planned the raid until he was back in his own lines only twenty minutes had elapsed and neither he nor his men had fired a shot. News of this raid spread throughout the Australian divisions and General Birdwood joined in the praise.

It was at this high point of morale that the Australian Corps was placed under Australian command for the first time. The new GOC was John Monash, in succession to Birdwood who was himself promoted to command the Fifth Army, superseding General Gough, who caught the blame for the German near-breakthrough. It was probably unfair to saddle Gough with this disaster but he had already done enough to prove himself a failure as a senior commander.

Some officers believed that Brudenell White, by then a major general, should have been appointed Australian Corps commander but, despite his brilliant record, he was junior to Monash in appointment. Birdwood took White with him as Fifth Army Chief of General Staff, while Monash appointed Brigadier T. A. Blamey as his Chief of Corps staff. At the same time the last two British divisional commanders in the Australian Corps, Major Generals H. B. Walker and N. M. Smyth, were transferred back to the British Army. As a major general, the forthright T. W. Glasgow took over the 1st Division, while Major General John Gellibrand succeeded Monash in command of the 3rd.

One sour note marred the change-over to Australian command of the AIF. Birdwood was given the odd post of 'administrative commander' of the AIF. It was the British High Command's last effort to retain a degree of control over Australian decisions and appointments. Fortunately, Birdwood had the good sense to suggest, rather than order, and he did not interfere with Monash's organisation.

Quite without premeditation, the scene had been set for the operation at Hamel, which was to become the Australians' most significant battle.

CHAPTER 6

Preparations for Battle

The military thinking which led to the Battle of Hamel had been a long time in the mental digestive process. Each time their divisions suffered heavy casualties for no appreciable gain, the Australian generals and brigadiers — who would themselves become generals — considered again what might be done to reduce the losses in men while at the same time securing a significant victory for themselves. This process had continued through 1916 and 1917 and into early 1918.

Brudenell White had the most acute mind in the upper echelons of the AIF, and he felt the losses even more keenly than most of his contemporaries. His chief, Birdwood, was a thoughtful, feeling general, but having grown up in the British school of military thought he found it impossible to intervene strongly in the councils attended by corps and army commanders and Haig himself. A graduate of the Royal Military Academy at Sandhurst, during the same period as some of the generals who were now his equals or superiors, he had the silent deference to superior rank which had always permeated the British Army. He could never be an effective questioner of the planning and conduct of operations. He may have wanted to do so but he was a member of the 'army establishment', which demanded a 'close-ranks' obedience to authority.

Monash had no difficulty in assuming the rule of AIF Corps commander and his own Australian contemporaries had no hesitation in accepting him as their chief. The man, Monash, the moment — a period of stalemate — and the place, Hamel, had come together.

In peacetime, the hamlet of Hamel had a population of only a few hundred people, most of them farmworkers whose families had lived there for generations. Some of these people had clung to their homes and tended their crops despite the war raging in France but the German Army's onslaught of March–April 1918 ended civilian occupation. The artillery of the Allies and the Germans wrecked all the buildings but Hamel was not reduced to brickdust and matchwood as Pozières had been, and the Germans had managed to incorporate what remained of the settlement into their front line.

In the middle of 1918 this line was a salient — a dent in what was a fairly straight British–Australian front line. It was a small but valuable salient for the Germans because behind the village itself was rising ground — and the Germans knew all about the importance of high ground. They had held it right along the Western Front throughout the war, with dire consequences for the Allies, whose leaders appeared to know no other tactic than to charge headlong against the powerful enemy emplacements. German defences at Hamel were in strong positions because just south of the village were terraces where, in ordinary times, fruit trees had been cultivated. These terraces made ideal sites for the Germans' Maxim machine-guns and their élite crews.

Behind the terraces was even higher ground, heavily wooded. This meant that the defenders could supply their forward posts without being seen. Also, in front of the terraces — that is, facing towards the Australians — were some shallow folds in the ground; here other gunpits and trenches had been dug where any attackers could not see them.

For two kilometres or more the Germans had an unrestricted field of fire across flat, open country. In daylight, no Allied activity was hidden from German observers.

In May, Rawlinson proposed the seizure of Hamel by the AIF 5th Division as a feint to draw the enemy's attention from south of Villers-Bretonneux, where a joint British–French attack was planned. Monash had also urged capture of Hamel at this time in order to protect the 3rd Division's right flank on the Somme River. Rawlinson revealed that the French had stated that they were making their offensive south of Villers-Bretonneux only if the Hamel feint were made. Once again Brudenell White demonstrated his moral courage. He said: 'If we have to carry out a perfectly useless attack at the cost of a division which it is desirable not to waste, there seems to me something very wrong in our arrangements'. This was a forthright objection from a 'mere' brigadier to a general, but the Hamel feint did not take place — that is, not as a mere feint.

The situation changed when Major General Charles Rosenthal's 2nd

Division had good results in their operations at Morlancourt and Sailly-Laurette, north of the Somme River. His line was now well ahead of that held by Major General E. G. Sinclair-MacLagan's 4th Division across the river to the south. Dangerously so — for German guns in Accroche Wood, near Hamel, were enfilading Rosenthal's flank and even firing on it from the rear. He refused to press further along the Corbie–Bray road and take even more artillery attack against his rear, and Monash admitted the rightness of this refusal. Another factor intervened: High Command wanted more space to defend the Villers-Bretonneux plateau, which was considered vital for the defence of Amiens. To attack the Germans was considered impossible while they held Hamel spur.

Monash now thought that capturing this key position was probably the most important operation that the Australian Corps could undertake, but he would need six infantry battalions while artillery movements would require several days. Reluctantly, he reported that he could not carry out the operation 'at present'.

The next development on the Hamel front came out of the blue. The 5th Tank Brigade, supporting the Fourth Army, had completed its change to the Mark V tank. The Mark V could move at only 5 mph (8 km/h) but this was 1 mph faster than the Mark IV; it was easier to drive and immeasurably more manoeuvrable. Major General Hugh Elles, commander of the Tank Corps, a born lobbyist and enthusiastic about his machines, approached many generals and brigadiers and sent his senior subordinates on similar missions. Elles' claim was persuasive: 'We can so greatly increase the capacity of infantry and artillery that we can decisively defeat the Germans before winter'. Monash and his chief-of-staff, Brigadier Tom Blamey, were invited to watch the new tanks demonstrate their abilities and they were greatly impressed.

Monash said that he proposed to undertake the Hamel operation if he had the assistance of tanks and if the Fourth Army would give him some more guns and improved 'air resources'.

We now come to a point of controversy. Lieutenant Colonel J. F. C. Fuller, another tank pioneer, had been given General Rawlinson as his 'target for tank conversion' and he was successful. Rawlinson no longer doubted the tanks' potential. On 18 June he wrote: 'I visited the Australian Corps today and proposed to Monash and MacLagan, with two battalions of tanks against Hamel village and the spur, to improve our position north of Villers-Bretonneux'.

Who first had the idea, Monash or Rawlinson? Bean wrote that the two generals had the idea simultaneously. Whatever the truth, it is certain — according to P. A. Pedersen — that Monash's enthusiasm for the new tanks far 'exceeded that of his Army commander and his divisional generals'.

The French general Mangin had attacked with 144 tanks on the Matz front, east of Villers Cotterets, on 14 June. But neither Rawlinson nor Monash appear to have heard of the success. British GHQ made no reference to it. It seems unlikely that Mangin's tank triumph influenced the Hamel operation in any way.

There could hardly be a better place than Hamel for such an attack, if only because the terrain was friendly and the Germans would not be able to see approaching tanks and infantry, being shielded by a spur which Sinclair-MacLagan's troops held. Furthermore, such an operation could not be outflanked because the left of the Australian line was protected by the River Somme.

Monash found a co-operative partner in Brigadier A. Courage, commanding the 5th Tank Brigade. The two men discussed their options and on 20 June Courage sent Monash his tank plan, which made use of Colonel Fuller's tanks doctrine. Four companies of tanks, in three groups and sixty in all, would make the attack. The fifteen tanks of the first section would force their way through the enemy lines to the rear, thus demoralising the Germans and blocking reinforcements. Then twenty-one tanks of Main Body, as Courage called the formation, would lead the infantry right onto their objectives. A 'mopping-up section' of nine tanks would crush remaining German opposition and replace any other machines knocked out. In a very real way, the four supply tanks were the most important of all. Originally built as mobile platforms for massive 60-pounder guns, these monsters could carry an immense quantity of stores, ammunition and equipment that would otherwise have to be taken up on the shoulders of weary men. Monash wanted no such delay.

In rehearsals and trials, it was found that a single tank, in one trip, could carry 134 coils of barbed wire, 180 long and 270 short screw pickets on which the wire was laced, forty-five sheets of corrugated iron to be used as trench covering, fifty petrol tins filled with water, 130 trench mortar bombs, 10 000 rounds of rifle ammunition and thirty-four boxes of hand grenades. Infantry officers at a demonstration were amazed at the quantity of material that came out of the tank. With four monsters carrying as much as this, the weight of stores going up to the fighting men was colossal. And if the tanks could be promptly unloaded they could be back with another load within ninety minutes. It was calculated that 1200 men would have been needed to carry up the quantity of stores taken forward by the supply tanks. No calculation was possible about how many of those men would have been killed or wounded but experience in other battles showed that as many as 30 per cent of soldiers engaged on porterage duties became casualties.

Courage, naturally enough, regarded the Hamel operation as principally a tank attack. Elles, Courage, Fuller and others understood the importance of the tanks' mobility in a way that officers of other arms did not yet comprehend. The infantry were to exploit the opportunities given to them by the tanks while at the same time pointing out targets of opportunity which tank commanders with their limited eye-vision might not notice.

Monash, with his quick grasp of opportunities, did comprehend the new role of tanks, but he well knew that only infantry could capture and consolidate the ground captured. Like the Tank Corps leaders, Monash realised that the tanks were a shock weapon, even though they were no longer secret. The Germans had seen what they could do during the Battle of Cambrai on 20 November 1917, but on that occasion they had recovered from their initial shock and no British breakthrough occurred.

Before the war Monash had spent his militia regimental career as an artillery officer. The knowledge that he gained from this experience enabled him fully to understand the potential of firepower. Together with his experienced artillery commander, Major General W. A. Coxen, he planned to employ his artillery to cover every phase of the battle.

The beginning and end of the artillery barrage would be marked by 18-pounder field guns firing entirely with smoke shells. Smoke would also screen the flanks of the attack; the shells would be fired by trench mortars and 4.5-inch howitzers. Smoke-screening would continue for two hours.

At odd times, so as not to arouse suspicion, a battery firing 9.2-inch shells — really heavy ones — would create shell-holes in which the infantry could lie. These holes were mapped and charts were given to junior leaders.

Similarly, annotated air photographs were distributed liberally to officers and NCOs, showing the lifts of the gun barrage, as they successively targeted the enemy forward positions, the trench lines and the objectives. Lieutenant Colonel D. G. Marks of the 13th Battalion — aged only twenty-three — had a 'message map' issued to every man of his unit. It was a small map of the battlefield, with message blanks already printed on the back. One line stated: 'I am at ____'. Another: 'I can see ____ at position marked _____'. The soldier might fill in the blanks with 'enemy machine-guns' and following 'marked' he might enter 'MG'.

Monash knew from experience that artillery could get his infantry onto the first objective, but once German intelligence identified this objective their artillery would come into action and the inevitable result was huge casualties. Nowhere had this been more amply demonstrated than at Pozières in 1916, when fresh Australian divisions occupied the same captured trench only to be blown to pieces.

To prevent this happening again Monash had to counter the German guns. To this end his artillery plan emphasised secrecy and deception, both of which had been lamentably lacking in the earlier Allied battles. Monash and Coxen agreed that all fire used to range onto targets from gun positions to be employed in the attack would be concealed by a large volume of fire from positions that were *not* to be used in the attack. Known enemy gun positions were not engaged but recorded. This was a shrewd idea because the Germans would not consider moving guns from positions that had not been fired upon.

When a German battery's move to a new position was detected the Australian artillery continued to shell the old location occasionally, another shrewd deception. In this way a complete picture of the German artillery in range of Hamel was established; at the same time the Germans were given a false picture of the Australian artillery deployment and knowledge.

The weight of Australian artillery for a short front of six-and-a-half kilometres was considerable. First there were the guns of four Australian divisions and the Australian Corps heavy artillery. But this was not enough to satisfy Monash and Coxen. Coxen borrowed additional British and French heavy artillery for the period of the attack. He finished up with more than 600 guns, of which 200 would be used to smash the German artillery. Monash laid down the precise volumes of gunfire needed to deliver a crushing blow against the enemy. As a British historian puts it, 'The education of the Fourth Army commander [Rawlinson] continued apace' under Monash. This writer further states:

Rawlinson, not least thanks to the initiatives of Monash and Courage and the intervention of Blamey and MacLagan, was now developing methods of attack which stood a substantial chance of subduing — at a tolerable cost of his infantry — *whatever* defences the enemy placed in their path. The point needs to be stressed. Under the initial Hamel plan, as devised by Monash and accepted by Rawlinson, some German machine-gunners would almost certainly have survived the barrage and escaped the attention of the tanks. They could then have taken heavy toll of the infantry coming forward unprotected in the wake of the armoured vehicles. The amended plan denied the enemy even this opportunity.

In order to engage the infantry, the German machine-gun posts had to survive, in succession, a bombardment from 302 heavy guns, then a field artillery barrage and finally an assault delivered by tanks and infantry in close co-operation. It should be too destructive even for the brave, skilful and stubborn German machine-gunners.

Haig approved Monash's scheme on 25 June, but there were to be changes even after that. The AIF infantry brigadiers — Coxen of the artillery, Sinclair-MacLagan and Monash's own chief-of-staff, Blamey — all wanted an artillery barrage because they could not overcome their prejudice against tanks, which had so tragically failed the 4th Division at Bullecourt. Depending on the tanks, the 4th Division had attacked without a barrage, but on the first night the unreliable tanks failed to arrive and the following night they could not reach the enemy wire. Sinclair-MacLagan and the brigadiers had their way, with perhaps grudging consent by Monash and Rawlinson.

Pedersen claims that Monash's wisdom in listening to and giving way to the opinions of his subordinate leaders was as outstanding a feature of the Battle of Hamel as any other. But Monash was insistent about certain matters. Despite the fears of many tank commanders, he ordered that the tanks must follow the artillery barrage dead-level with the infantry, even though the huge tanks, nearly three metres in height, were vulnerable to artillery dropshorts — the 'friendly fire' of later generations. A potential source of confusion and disagreement was obviated by Monash's order that the infantry commander on the spot would give orders to the tank section commander 'as the situation demands'.

After the Bullecourt debacle, the Tank Corps men knew that they must gain the confidence of the Diggers, not just their senior officers. Every day the soldiers were transported by battalion to the tank-training ground at Vaux-en-Amienois. Here the crews took the infantrymen for what they called 'joy rides', but their purpose was earnestly clear: they proved that the tanks were reliable and they answered all of the many questions put to them. One asked by junior officers and NCOs was, 'How do we attract your attention in the tank?'

'Just ring the back-door bell,' they were told. At the rear of each fighting tank was a short bell rope which when yanked rang a bell inside. The tank commander would then open a hatch at the rear to listen to any request for tactical assistance.

But there were other more formal signals for the Hamel operation:

- tanks to infantry: red, white and blue flag = 'Coming out of action';
- infantry to tanks: tanks to infantry: red and yellow flags = 'Broken down'; and
- infantry to tanks: helmet placed on bayonet = 'Tanks wanted here'.

The Mark I tank had crawled at 3–5 kilometres an hour, took three men to drive, could not reverse, had to stop before it could turn and could be shot through with armour-piercing bullets. In the demonstrations at Vaux-en-Amienois, the Diggers saw the tanks moving almost as fast as running infantry, with single drivers turning them rapidly in any direction and backing them at will.

And there was more. Tank crews showed how they could hurry to an enemy machine-gun post which was holding up infantry and 'rub it out'. The monster machine would roll over such a post and then 'iron it' with pirouetting motions. The Australians saw that both the enemy gunners and their Maxims would be mangled and crushed.

Many soldiers were worried that, should they be wounded, especially amid long grass or crops, they could be run over by a tank. Visibility through the eye slits in the tank was limited and tank crews could not be expected, in the heat of battle, to see a man lying on the ground. This fear was allayed by an instruction distributed throughout the attacking force that should a soldier be wounded and disabled, one of his mates would stick the injured man's rifle in the ground close to him. In addition, pieces of white tape would be tied to the tops of crops to indicate the position of seriously wounded. In the event, these precautions ensured that no wounded were crushed by tanks and they greatly helped stretcher-bearers during their search for wounded men.

Most heartening of all to the watching troops was the tanks' demonstration of dealing with obstacles. Engineers had built strongpoints, dug deep trenches and erected swathes of barbed wire. Now the tank crews showed that they could crush all obstacles and roll over trenches. The Diggers' confidence in the tanks was immense after a day working with them.

During the battles of the Lys and Aisne, earlier in the year, German aircraft had dropped ammunition to their forward troops. Monash ordered that this would be done at Hamel. He used the developing air arm — which had changed its name from the Royal Flying Corps to the Royal Air Force in April — in various ways. Every officer and NCO in the attacking units was given recent aerial photographs. Each day as the plans proceeded, RAF scout aircraft flew over the Australian lines, artillery positions and tank forming-up areas to spot and report on any sign of movements and dispositions taken up during the preceding night. In this way it could be fairly certain that enemy spotters would see nothing important.

Monash wanted reports of progress to reach the operational commander, Sinclair-MacLagan, within minutes. Air observers were issued with map blanks and report pads; they marked on them the changing positions of Australian and enemy troops and dropped them in weighted and plumed canisters to motorcycle dispatch riders waiting at designated places. The Don Rs would then rush the information to HQ. At the time, this was the nearest thing possible to what later became 'real-time' intelligence.

The troops were issued with small flares that would fit into a packet not much larger than a cigarette box. When they occupied an enemy position, many men struck these flares simultaneously as a British observer aircraft flew over. Back at HQ Sinclair-MacLagan and Monash quickly knew what position their troops had reached.

Through Rawlinson, Monash obtained from Haig a squadron of Handley Page heavy bombers to target villages and woods where German reserves were known to be.

No. 9 Squadron RAF was standing by to drop ammunition to the fighting troops. Like everybody else involved in the Hamel operation, the fliers had practised for their task. Flying in line ahead — that is, one after another — they dropped two brown parachutes, each of them carrying a box of 1200 rounds of small-arms ammunition. Some drop sites were already arranged; the infantry would mark others with a white V sign. The squadron expected that each plane would make four trips during the day. Monash and his staff, through the supply tanks and aircraft, might be providing their troops with more ammunition than they needed, but this was preferable to the soldiers' having to ration their firing in case they should run out of cartridges.

Other RAF squadrons were detailed to seek out and strafe German batteries and parties of enemy infantry that might be hiding beyond the next hill eastwards, ready to reinforce the front. Aeroplanes of No. 3 Australian squadron had a double duty — observing as well as protecting when necessary the planes making the supply drops.

Not before in the war had aircraft been used in so many diverse ways.

While he had adequate artillery and armour, Monash was short of manpower. In common with every other corps on the Western Front, the Australian Corps was under strength, with a shortfall of 8000 men. Reinforcements were simply not available and already thought was being given to disbanding some battalions and incorporating the men thus obtained into other battalions. Monash was well aware that in Australia the public was in shock over the casualties the AIF had incurred. The prime minister, W. M. Hughes, was in Europe and he had told Monash of the public disquiet.

Monash needed no lectures about the avoidance of casualties. He held strong views about the reckless waste of infantry, which he had been witnessing for years. 'The role of infantry,' he wrote,

was not to expend itself upon heroic physical effort, not to wither away under merciless machine-gun fire, not to impale itself on hostile bayonets, but on the contrary, to advance under the maximum possible protection of the maximum possible array of mechanical resources in the form of guns, machine-guns, tanks, mortars and aeroplanes.

He and Major General Sinclair-MacLagan, GOC Fourth Division, who was to be the field commander for the operation, proposed to use only one brigade from each of the three AIF divisions then available. In this way any losses would not fall on just one division, as had so often happened during the previous two years. Two brigades would attack at Hamel and the third would make a diversionary attack north of the Somme River. A brigade might seem like a strong force, but losses had been heavy and Monash had only 7500 men for his Hamel operation.

The 4th and 11th Brigades would make the actual assault. The 4th consisted of the 13th, 14th, 15th and 16th Battalions. It was known as an all-states brigade since its units represented every state of the Commonwealth. The 11th Brigade's battalions came from Queensland, South Australia and Western Australia. The 14th Battalion was designated the support battalion for its brigade, while the 41st was the reserve battalion for the 11th Brigade.

The 11th Brigade was particularly weak; its casualties during enemy gas-shelling at Villers-Bretonneux in May had been serious. The 43rd Battalion had taken 230 casualties and had been re-organised into three companies, each of three platoons; normal strength was four or five companies with six or seven platoons.

The 21st and 23rd Battalions of the 8th Brigade were selected to carry out a diversionary attack north of the Somme River. This diversionary attack was important. While he had great resources in guns and tanks, Monash knew that a diversionary attack close to Hamel would not only confuse the German command but also stop it from sending units from north of the river to strengthen the Hamel front.

The AIF battalions were good but their ranks were depleted. The entire frontline strength of the 11th Brigade was ninety-nine officers and 1984 men, while the 4th Brigade was only a little stronger with about 2300. During the Battle of Cambrai in November 1917, two brigades on average had attacked on an 700-metre front. At Hamel, Monash was increasing this length of front fourfold, still with only two brigades. It could hardly be said of Hamel, as it was said of the Battle of Cambrai, that infantry were thick on the ground. Monash and Sinclair-MacLagan were making up for the lack of riflemen with the tanks and artillery strength. Even so, as a 'better to be safe than sorry' general, Monash would have preferred more infantry.

The idea for the use of American troops to add to the infantry strength at Hamel appears to have been that of Rawlinson. Why not, he asked, give the Americans, who were training with the Australians, the experience of taking part in a model set-piece attack, especially as the Australians were so highly skilled? Everybody had been impressed with the physique, enthusiasm and intelligence of the Americans and, in experienced company, they should perform well. The matter was mentioned to Monash, who asked for about 2000 men organised in eight companies.

General John Pershing, commanding the American Expeditionary Force, had wanted his army to have its own independent front. This was unrealistic. Eager and fit though the Americans were, they were still only half-trained and totally inexperienced. To have given the AEF its own front during the first half of 1918 would have invited a German attack with almost certain American defeat. Nevertheless, it was understandable that Pershing disliked the proposition that his units should form a ready reserve to reinforce weakened British and French formations. Nevertheless, on 17 June he apportioned two of his ten divisions to the BEF for training, while they held emergency positions behind the British Third and Fourth Armies. The 65th Brigade of the 33rd Division, from Illinois, was attached to the Australian Corps.

Rawlinson obtained Haig's permission to use some Americans in the Hamel attack but he did not approach Pershing, perhaps already fearing a negative reaction. Instead, he took his request to Major General G. Bell, GOC 33rd Division, and Major General G. W. Read, commanding the US II Corps. They too did not consult their chief, but they detailed two companies from each of the 131st and 132nd Regiments. An American company was 250-strong, more than double that of a British or Australian company; a platoon numbered seventy, also more than double the strength of an AIF platoon. Monash got only 1000 of the 2000 men he had asked for but another six companies later joined the Australians.

In the American system, the infantry battalions had fewer officers than the AIF, with considerable authority given to master sergeants (the equivalent to an Australian sergeant major) and sergeants.

Colonel J. B. Sanborn of the 131st Regiment, reported, 'There were great manifestations of joy when the order for action with the Australians was received. Sending off his troops one commander told his men, "You will be fighting along with lads who always deliver the goods".'

The troops marched at once to join the AIF. The 131st joined the 11th AIF Brigade, then resting in the woods at Allonville, while the 132nd Regiment men reached the 4th Brigade, in bivouac near Aubigny, close to the Somme River bank. The Australians, having learnt that the Yanks were not braggarts but keen learners, welcomed the newcomers. An American lieutenant, F. L. Rinkliff, noted that the three platoons of the 42nd Battalion's company which he joined were depleted to fewer than twenty-six men. 'But all have the appearance of fighting men,' he wrote.

In every aspect of planning, the staff work by Monash's team was exemplary. That carried out by Major S. A. Hunn, a wool-classer in civil life, was of special importance. Hunn was Monash's chief of intelligence and he gave his general an appreciation of the enemy position and the strength with which it was held. From information given by prisoners and reports by Australian patrols and air observers, Hunn estimated the German strength at 2790, with 2860 in reserve. This was not an alarming number and, stated Hunn, they came from divisions which had only mediocre reputations.

He told Monash and Sinclair-MacLagan that Hamel Wood and Vaire Wood were strongly fortified and well supplied with machine-guns. Elsewhere, the wire protection was thin, while the trenches were shallow and ineptly co-ordinated. Hunn was sure that the Germans could not readily form a new front when driven out of their first lines.

As part of the overall intelligence program, secrecy about the impending attack was essential. As little as possible was committed to paper. So often in the past, NCOs and officers had been taken prisoner with valuable information in their pockets or packs.

Major Hunn knew that the Germans were equally guilty of such indiscretions and he wanted to avoid it with his own troops at Hamel. He did not have to convince Monash, who depended on 'conferences' to exchange and discuss plans and to give instructions. The need for secrecy and creative deception cropped up frequently.

For Monash the planner, conferences were paramount and he ordered that every officer who 'mattered' would attend any given conference. He knew exactly which officers should be there and he made a mental check of those present. Each key officer was called upon to explain his plans to the conference and, if necessary, defend them. Monash wrote that when any conflict or doubt or difference of opinion occurred, he or the relevant senior officer present gave a 'final and unalterable' decision on the spot. After that no deviation was permitted. He had witnessed many dangers and some terrible disasters in deviations from orders, such as the unilateral decision at Fromelles of a British general to cancel an attack which left the Australians on his left flank exposed to German attack from their rear. Many other disasters had been caused by failure to hold a conference, as at Bullecourt in 1917.

Before Hamel, a major conference took place on 28 June, at which Monash presented an agenda of 118 items. At the final pre-Hamel conference on 30 June the corps commander's agenda listed 133 items and the meeting lasted four-and-a-half hours. It may have left some of the 250 officers weary, even bored, but none could have left the meeting wondering if he had understood everything. All of them had learnt, too, that they could ask questions without being made to look foolish or incompetent. At conferences called by British commanders and attended by senior high-ranking Australians, a meeting usually ended with the presiding officer saying briskly, 'Any questions? No, good. Then that will be all today gentlemen'.

After 30 June there was no need for a corps commander's conference on Hamel, but the operational chief, brigade and battalion commanders, having been set a model by Monash, held briefing sessions which were attended not only by officers but also by key NCOs, such as the RSM, the RQMS, the senior Medical Corps sergeants, CSMs and, at battalion level, many others.

On 2 July Pershing learned about the battle. He did not approve and he told Rawlinson so. Rawlinson passed on his objection to Haig, who ordered that the Americans be withdrawn. On 3 July all but four companies were marched out. The men were greatly distressed and there were stories that some of them dressed in Australian uniforms in order to take part in the coming battle.

At 4 pm on 3 July a bombshell hit Monash: Rawlinson informed him that the final four American companies were also to be taken out. Monash, angry and exasperated, retorted that it was already too late to make this move. He gave Rawlinson an ultimatum: if the Americans did not participate he would abandon the attack. Moreover, he wanted a firm decision by 6.30 pm when the troops would begin their final approach to the startline, ready for imminent battle. Rawlinson was shocked and pleaded with Monash. If the attack did not proceed, he told Monash, Haig might relieve him, Rawlinson, of command.

Monash was unmoved. Curtly, he told Rawlinson that co-operation between the Australians and Americans in this battle was more important than the career even of an army commander who might have aspirations to become Commander-in-Chief. He also knew, but did not say, that it was more important to take this opportunity to demonstrate Australian senior leadership — probably the best chance he would get — than to save Rawlinson's career.

Monash's insistence on American participation was justified purely on numerical grounds, but for him there was another factor. He told Rawlinson that if the Americans did not take part, after enthusiastic Australian acceptance of them, that in future the Australians, as soldiers and as a nation, would never trust the Americans again. It was not their fault that they were to be taken out, but history would see it as their fault. It seems possible to me that Monash had an eye on the future.

This display of moral courage — virtually defiance of his army commander and the commander-in-chief — was Monash at his strongest. In the British Army, with juniors afraid of their seniors and almost in awe of the C-in-C, Monash's stand was truly remarkable. He went further: he set a deadline by which he wanted a favourable decision. Unless he received approval to employ his Americans, the Hamel attack was off.

Embarrassed and in near panic about incurring Haig's displeasure, Rawlinson ordered that the operation go ahead as planned, including the

Americans, unless contrary orders were received from Haig by Monash's set time. They did not arrive by 6.30 pm and, at Rawlinson's urgent request, Monash gave Haig another half hour. Blamey and the others senior members of Monash's staff knew that he was in deadly earnest. The minutes ticked by as the staff prepared to issue STOP orders to the field commanders. At 6.58 Haig's approval for the four American companies to participate in the battle came through. Rawlinson was immensely relieved. Haig, too, had realised that Monash was not bluffing. He now said that the improvement in the line in front of Amiens was vital and the operation must proceed. Monash had got his way.

Despite the meticulous planning, the exhaustive conferences and briefings, it was in the very nature of war that something would go wrong. Emergencies could be planned for but not entirely foreseen. By example, precept and command, by patience with his junior subordinates, trust with his senior subordinates — the major generals and brigadiers — and firmness with his own superiors, Monash was ready to go. He was so confident that, only hours before the many disparate elements of his operation began to move, he told his artillery commander, Coxen, that only one happening could now deny him victory at Hamel: if the Germans were to discover his plan and open a massive artillery barrage to thwart it.

His famous description is worth repeating: 'A perfected modern battle plan is like nothing so much as a score for an orchestral composition, where the various arms and units are the instruments, and the tasks they perform are the respective musical phrases'.

The composer-conductor Monash had not long to wait for the music to begin.

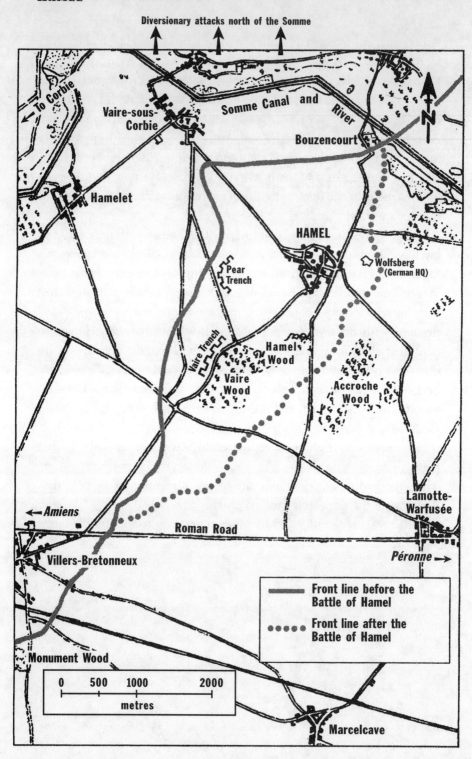

Diversionary attacks north of the Somme

To Corbie

Vaire-sous-
Corbie

Somme Canal and River

Bouzencourt

Hamelet

HAMEL

Pear
Trench

Wolfsberg
(German HQ)

Vaire Trench

Hamel
Wood

Vaire
Wood

Accroche
Wood

Lamotte-
Warfusée

Amiens

Roman Road

Péronne

Villers-Bretonneux

⸻⸻ Front line before the
Battle of Hamel

•••••• Front line after the
Battle of Hamel

Monument Wood

0   500   1000   2000

metres

Marcelcave

70

CHAPTER 7

Into Battle

Much confusing, contradictory and ignorant comment has been made about the German defences at Hamel. By some accounts, including pre-battle intelligence reports, the German wire was thin and the trenches shallow, 'barely scratched out' in places. Parapets were inefficiently constructed and the defensive system was poorly laid out.

But much incidental and narrative evidence suggests the contrary, that the enemy position was strong and in places dauntingly formidable. The tank leaders' plan specified that the tanks, with infantry support, were to 'overcome strongpoints and mop up trenches'. Elsewhere, in C. E. W. Bean's *Official History* for example, we are told that the heavy tanks 'flattened whole lines of trenches, weapon pits and shelters'. This description indicates positions of strength.

We know, too, that the Germans had occupied the old French-built Amiens defence line and had strengthened many small weapon pits and communication trenches.

In the *Official History*, battalion histories and personal accounts — such as in *Jacka's Mob* by E. J. Rule — there are numerous references to deep dugouts. From some of them as many as sixty or seventy prisoners were taken. So the dugouts were deep and large; further indication of strong positions. The German defences were undoubtedly on the brow of the ridge beyond Hamel, especially on the right, in Accroche Wood, from where the enemy had good visibility and a fine field of fire.

Undoubtedly, too, some enemy trenches were shallow and in places the barbed wire was thin, but this is not evidence of weak defences. The Germans had excellent trenches; the shallow ones had been abandoned because officers had noted that trenches would be better in other places. The thin wire was intended to delay and divert, not necessarily to stop.

Any realistic account of the German defences must begin with the machine-guns. The German Maxims infested the Hamel position, as they did in many parts of the Western Front. At Hamel they were in special weapon pits, in the trenches, spaced in lines along the terraces on the left of Hamel village, and in camouflaged positions, especially near the woods. Over and over again machine-guns held up the Australian advance and inflicted many casualties. Whatever defects any defensive system had, if it was well supplied with expertly sited machine-guns, it was powerful. And the officers and NCOs of the élite German Machine-Gun Corps were experts.

The defenders of Hamel inflicted nearly 1400 casualties on the Australians and about one hundred on the Americans. A weak defensive system could not have caused such a loss. The loss was small when compared with the grotesquely huge losses in large battles, but in absolute numbers 1400 men killed or wounded out of an attacking force of 7000 averages one casualty for every five men.

My best witness to the strength of the German defences at Hamel is Major (later Colonel) Burford Sampson of the 15th Battalion, who fought at Hamel. He records in his diary that on 10 July, in the company of the battalion intelligence officer, he inspected parts of the battlefield. 'Had a good look around Vaire Wood and Central Copse,' he wrote. 'Hun position one of great natural strength — splendid field of fire and well concealed. Three distinct fire positions and numerous M.W. emplacements. [MW stood for minniewerfer, the German mortar.] Great quantities of MG [machine-gun] ammo.'

To speak of the German positions at Hamel as weak is not merely misleading, it is false. Any man who has been an infantry soldier can see at a glance that in German hands the natural fortress-like aspects of the terrain would have been made virtually impregnable.

Major Sampson had good reason to know about the strength of the Germans at Hamel. His 15th Battalion went into the attack with twenty-one officers and 615 other ranks. Its losses were nine officers and 231 men, the highest by far of any battalion engaged; that is, practically one man in three became a casualty.

Sampson's battalion captured thirty-seven machine-guns. This number of Maxims on the front of a single battalion is proof that the enemy defences were strong. That the Diggers of the 15th Battalion could kill, wound, capture or drive out the defenders against such a volume of firepower is also proof of skill, determination and courage. Those historians who write about the 'weak' German defences at Hamel are grossly undervaluing the achievements of the Diggers who fought there.

The infantry action at Hamel began at 3.10 am on 4 July but Monash's tactics had already softened up the Germans and deceived them. For days the Australian and British artillery had been treating the Germans to a harassing fire, a mixture of high explosives, gas and smoke. The Germans assumed that this gunfire was merely to torment them and not to attempt to annihilate them before an infantry assault. Putting on their gas masks, they went to sleep in their deeper dugouts. Not that sleep came easily because British aircraft flew along and across their lines in the darkness. They made as much noise as possible to deprive the Germans of sleep and to accustom them to the anticipation that the air activity was unrelated to any enemy ground action.

From 1 July onwards Australian engineers placed a pontoon bridge across the Somme between Vaux and Vaire. It helped the traffic of artillery and ammunition columns to move forward during the night, when the roads were crowded with troops and vehicles. Before daylight the Engineers took the bridge apart so the enemy would not see it, but they put in place a bridge which was designed to draw fire away from the real crossings. An angry battery commander said that this phoney bridge was bringing fire on his nearby guns and demolished it. The genuine bridge was also meant for stretcher-bearers bringing back wounded but it was not put in place until after dark on 3 July.

Field reconnaissance had been continuing during the pre-battle period. Two days before fighting began scout officers from various units arrived to live in the line. Their reconnaissances showed that the enemy was comparatively close on the right flank, with No-Man's-Land 230 metres wide. From that direction the German machine-gunners were active. On the left flank No-Man's-Land was as much as 650 metres across and the Germans were not particularly aggressive. In No-Man's-Land opposite Notamel Wood the crops were high, an advantage for troops quietly approaching their start line.

Unit intelligence officers and their small sections laid the white tape start lines after dark on 3 July. They were easily found by the slowly assembling troops but could not be seen by the Germans, even by those on the higher ground behind the village of Hamel. The intelligence officers also had the task of cutting their own wire so that the infantry could pass through it.

At a high point on the eastern edge of the village of Vaire-sous-Corbie, platoon commanders arrived one at a time to study the ground and note any landmarks. Enemy observers would have been suspicious had they seen a large number of men arriving at any one time.

On the night of the battle, several unit commanders saw to it that their men had an extra hot meal about midnight and later a tot of warming rum, though this was contrary to AIF practice, which was to issue rum only after an action. The Americans were surprised and delighted by the late meal and they were intrigued when their Australian mates after eating lay down on the start line and fell asleep. Most of the inexperienced Americans were too tense to sleep.

There were some approach problems. For instance, the intelligence sections missed some lengths of barbed wire and the troops had to pick their way through it. The abominable Australian puttees often snagged the barbs but the Americans, wearing canvas gaiters, had no such problem.

In one place on the 11th Brigade's front, the troops were given a last-minute order to pull back fifty yards until they could be certain where their own barrage would drop. Most guns had not been ranged, as this could have alerted the nervous Germans to anticipate an attack, and much therefore depended on the gunners being exact in their calculations.

The night was remarkably quiet and peaceful, despite so much movement on the field of battle; in reports and diaries some officers commented on the eerie silence.

For two weeks the gunners had been treating the Germans to the usual pre-dawn harassing fire and, at 3.02 am on 4 July, they began this routine with a mixture of high explosive, gas and smoke shells. Under cover of this racket, the tanks, half a mile behind the front, began a full-speed approach. They needed twelve minutes to reach the Australian infantry. To the AIF commanders, the noise seemed fearful and sure to alarm the enemy, but the gunfire, together with aeroplane noise, covered the tanks' clank and clatter. The RAF's No. 101 Squadron, flying old FE planes with howling engines, was particularly effective on its 'noise patrol'.

Between dusk and dawn the fliers dropped 350 25-pound bombs.

The Germans still expected no danger, though one of their guns fired a parachute flare which hovered brilliantly above the British tanks. For two minutes everybody was tense, but obviously the tanks were not seen for no gunfire followed the flare.

The surprise barrage began at 3.10. The eighty 6-inch guns and the twenty 8-inch and 9.2-inch howitzers fired 600 yards ahead of the infantry; the 4.5-inch howitzers dropped their shells 400 yards ahead while the shells of the 18-pounders exploded 200 yards in front. The troops had been ordered to follow the bursting shells, which would creep ahead of them, at a distance of seventy-five yards. They had been assured that if they kept to this distance they would not be hit by their own shells.

It was not that simple. Unable to range their guns before the battle, the gunners had been forced to calculate their distance by studying maps, a difficult exercise for many soldiers. At several parts of the line guns fired short. By coincidence, this occurred at the junction of the 4th and 11th Brigades. Shells exploded among them. Opposite the Germans' Pear Trench, the 15th Battalion was also caught by 'own gunfire' — the grotesque term 'friendly fire' would not appear for another fifty years. The 15th lost twelve men killed instantly and another thirty wounded, even before the battalion was in action.

There was no way of reaching these defaulting guns with orders to cease fire or to raise their range, and they continued to drop short throughout the battle. The platoon leaders of the 'victimised' troops managed to adjust their advance to the actual drop of shells rather than to the theoretical fall.

Elsewhere, the inexperienced Americans, desperately eager to be good soldiers and impress their new Australian mates, pressed much too close to their own barrage. Corporal Mick Roach of the 13th Battalion spotted a platoon of Americans entering the burst zone and ran ahead of them, shouting and waving at them to stop. He lost his life in this gallant action. When an American officer was badly wounded, Sergeant F. J. Darke took over his platoon and, risking his life, succeeded in halting the bewildered men. Luck was with him and he was not hurt. Michael Roach, aged 35, is buried in Villers-Bretonneux Military Cemetery.

Not one tank had yet been spotted by the anxious infantry and, with painful memories of Bullecourt, many Australians wondered at this point if the tanks had let them down again. In fact, in the dark and smoke the tank commanders had great difficulty in finding their way. Meanwhile, that same smoke and dust gave the troops the cover from enemy sight that they needed, if not from small-arms fire.

The tank officers, who would have preferred a later start, were doing their best. Many commanders got out of their tanks and led the way by compass direction while in the conning tower a crew member or an Australian scout did his best to keep the officer in sight.

The 43rd Battalion was probably in action first, meeting opposition about 300 metres from the first advance. Enemy machine-guns opened up, killing Lieutenant F. R. Brook and wounding several men. The fire stopped Brook's platoon, shaken by the early loss of its leader, but Corporal F. M. Shaw and an American, Corporal H. G. Zyburt, rushed the post, Shaw firing his Lewis gun from the hip. Under this torrent of fire Zyburt bayoneted three of the German crew, though he himself was wounded.

The aggressive Shaw looked around for other work and spotted a machine-gun and its crew behind a bank. Unseen, he advanced to within 100 metres of the post, and Lewis gun at the hip hosed it with bullets. Gunners fell, but when Shaw was thirty metres away a German officer rushed at him firing a revolver. This brave man also died. One German remained alive as Shaw reached the gun and he showed fight until Shaw, his magazine empty, hit him on the head and then shot him. Eight enemy now lay dead in the post and the casing of their Maxim was riddled with Shaw's bullets. This one-man assault was remarkably daring and Diggers who watched it were amazed that the corporal had emerged from it unwounded.

Shaw stayed lucky. A little later in the battle, beyond the village, he was present when three machine-guns in a quarry opened up on men of the 43rd. A tank was signalled to come up and it drove over two of the guns, forcing the crews into a dugout. Meanwhile Shaw led a few men in an attack on the third, which he captured, taking prisoner seventeen Germans.

In all, Shaw fired nine magazines throughout the operation and proved the value of the Lewis gun in the hands of a brave and determined man. Inexplicably, Shaw was not awarded the VC although his feats were the equal of many actions which were considered to merit one, and even more sustained. He was given the lesser DCM.

The 43rd's centre company commander, Captain H. S. Cope, met fierce resistance at the western edge of Hamel. Under fire and as yet without tank support, most Diggers lay flat and fired while others were ordered to throw or bowl bombs. Nothing made an impression on the enemy soldiers behind a long, wide and low heap of turnips, and Cope was reluctant to order a frontal charge which would certainly be costly.

Calling to Lieutenant J. G. Symons, he ordered him to lead his platoon of Americans in an outflanking attack. This disconcerted the Germans, enabling the men under Cope and Symons combined to make a rush. They killed fifteen enemy and captured forty. With Symons wounded, Private D. J. Anderson, the only other experienced soldier, took command and led the platoon in clearing Hamel. Without hesitation, the American officer and NCOs followed and obeyed this private soldier who was obviously a veteran at his job.

The hardest fighting of the battle fell to the 15th Battalion and especially to those platoons on the unit's left. Because of short shooting by the guns, the troops could get no closer to the main barrage than 200 metres. This meant that the Diggers were not well protected and German machine-guns were able to fire at them, causing casualties. Also, enemy grenades were reaching them. Captain E. K. Carter, commanding at this point, had both legs broken but his men ran towards the enemy bombers. They were making for Pear Trench but they found it protected by rolls of wire which the gunfire had not cut. While some men climbed over the obstacle, others fought their way through it.

Fire from Pear Trench was heavy enough to check the approach of other 15th Battalion men. Three tanks had been specifically detailed to roll over the Pear Trench objective but the infantry officers on the spot could not wait for them. This was a time for what the Australian infantry did so well — fire and movement. The two Lewis gun crews of each platoon could see no target when they lay down in the tall crops, so the gunners stood and sprayed their bullets from the hip. This at least unsettled the German Maxim gunners. Captain Carter's men silenced two guns and rushed the positions, but on the left a third Maxim opened up.

By now only one Australian Lewis team, under Private Henry Dalziel, was still in action. He slapped a fresh drum of cartridges onto the gun which his mate was firing. Then, revolver in hand, Dalziel rushed the enemy post. He shot two Germans and captured the gun, but he spared a third German because, as he said later, 'The youngster fought so well'. Dalziel himself was twenty-five.

In the continuing fighting Dalziel's trigger finger was shot away and blood flowed copiously from the wound. An officer ordered him to the rear but he pretended he had not understood and followed up the attack. He ignored a second order to report to an aid post. Unable to hold a weapon, he made himself useful by bringing up a box of ammunition dropped from an aeroplane and while doing this he was shot in the head. He survived and was awarded the VC.

Pear Trench contained many machine-guns and some mortar pits. The enemy soldiers clung to positions behind Pear and one steady gunner continued to fire until the Diggers reached him and bayoneted him. By now some enemy had their hands up in surrender but from behind them others went on throwing bombs. The Diggers, who had suffered heavily, saw this as 'white-flag treachery' and now killed without compunction. An American captain, G. H. Mallon, counted forty dead in 'a very small sector'. The enraged troops were not interested in the fine point that as no official surrender under a recognised leader had taken place, it was legally permissible for men to go on firing even though their comrades had put their hands up. To the Queenslanders at Pear that day, some of them splashed by the blood of their mates, it did not matter whether hands were up or not.

Having cleared the area, the 15th met no further opposition and when they reached the designated ten-minutes halt line they sat or stood about smoking cigarettes, which they were doing when their tanks came up.

The 15th's commanding officer, Lieutenant Colonel T. P. McSharry, was as tough a soldier as any of his men but he did not kill indiscriminately. He had found several Germans in mortar pits and saw that they were feigning death in an attempt to escape. McSharry threw earth clods at them, at which they 'came alive' and surrendered.

The 16th Battalion, flanking the 15th on the right, came up against strong opposition from the second recognised obstacle in front of Vaire and Hamel Woods. Here the Germans had machine-guns spaced along commanding terraces, with the strongest post at Kidney Trench, which was protected by wire. One gun team caused near havoc.

In sustained bursts of fire they seriously wounded a company commander, Captain F. E. Woods, and his sergeant major, H. G. Blinman; both died a few hours later. Wiping out a Lewis gun crew, the enemy gunners checked the 16th's attack.

Lance Corporal Tom Axford was a little way behind this carnage, but now he ran to the front and threw his grenades at the enemy machine-gun crew. Before the bombs had burst he jumped into the trench, where he killed ten Germans. He shouted at the six men who had survived his onslaught to clear out and gestured to the Australians' rear. Heaving the heavy captured Maxim gun onto the trench parapet, he yelled to his platoon, 'Come on!'. Spellbound by Axford's actions, his platoon briskly followed him. Minutes later they captured forty-seven Germans in dugouts in a sunken road.

Axford's one-man attack was clearly a VC exploit and in due course this twenty-four-year-old miner from Coolgardie was awarded the decoration.

With Captain Woods gone, command of his company fell to Lieutenant J. B. Minchin, formerly a private in the same company and its cook. Promoted, he had proved a splendid leader and had already been awarded the MC. Now he led his line of riflemen and Lewis gunners towards and into the woods. Firing from the hip, they forced the enemy troops into the Australian barrage, which felled some of them. At the north-east corner of Hamel Wood, a platoon strengthened by stretcher-bearers and orderlies stubbornly clung to a company headquarters. A tank was signalled up to deal with this obstacle but before it could arrive a phosphorus bomb set fire to a fortified dugout and incinerated several Germans. This horror was enough to cause the rest to surrender.

Throughout the fight, enemy machine-gunners were the main opposition. Where they were allowed to remain in action they caused casualties. For instance, on the 42nd Battalion's front, two Maxims killed or wounded nine Diggers and were holding up the advance. Again a tank was called up and while it overwhelmed one gun Lance Corporal Daley, a Lewis gunner, outflanked the other gun and rushed in to kill the crew.

The élite soldiers of the German Machine-Gun Corps rarely ran from their guns, even when in dire peril. Bean quotes Colonel D. Bingham of the Tank Corps as saying that, in general, the German machine-gun crews 'showed extraordinary courage and tenacity and refused to surrender until completely wiped out or run over by a tank'. This might have been better expressed. If the Germans were wiped out and run over, the question of surrender was an irrelevance.

Despite the stiff resistance at certain points, the Germans had been taken by surprise and many of them were wearing gas masks when captured, proof that Monash's daily morning mix of gas, smoke and high explosive had done its intended work of deceiving the Germans into thinking that no infantry assault would follow the gas. Another of Monash's tactics had worked.

As pre-arranged, some battalion HQs sent messages to the rear by rockets. Somebody on Monash's staff had considered the experiment worthwhile. One rocket fell within yards of a reporting station but most dropped wild and often in crops where they could not be seen. At one point the 43rd Battalion signalled by Lucas lamp from a tree. As early as 5.30 am 4th Brigade HQ was in touch by telephone and signallers kept the landline intact, even under shellfire. The first messages from officers on the objective were passed by wireless, which was revolutionary in warfare at that time.

One task which fell to the 44th Battalion was to capture a whole complex of trenches on and over the ridge crest. With the help of tanks, the 44th took one Maxim position after another. On these heights the dugouts were well built and many enemy soldiers were in them. The 44th captured fifty men in one dugout and forty in another. Among them was a major with the men of his battalion headquarters. In yet another trench the 44th captured fifty men and twenty-seven light machine-guns.

The task of the 13th Battalion was to encircle Vaire Wood once the 16th had cleared it and to capture the final objective, a spur of ground. Only an experienced battalion with fit and disciplined men under skilful leaders would have carried out the complex manoeuvres involved. Part of the battalion doubled around the southern edge of the wood and then up behind it, aiming to link with the right of the 15th Battalion coming from the other direction. One company dug in as planned while the two companies behind it ran northwards as fast as possible. Inexperienced running soldiers quickly lose cohesion, but the men of the 13th remained in formation. The fourth company went straight on.

Bean described how the men of the 13th Battalion companies had been told to use Rugby football tactics. Vaire Wood was the scrum; they had to double round it as a scrum half-back would do, and head for the corner 500 metres to the north. Here they turned east — that is, into German territory — and advanced in line again.

Commanding the northward rush was Captain G. Harper, who had been a sergeant under Captain Harry Murray, VC, and in 1916 had fought at Mouquet Farm, among other places. When an enemy machine-gun crew which had stuck to their post opened fire on Harper's company he charged it alone, shot three Germans and captured the gun. After this very brief diversion, he was turning his line of Diggers eastwards to complete the manoeuvre when his rush was stopped dead by two machine-guns in a trench so well hidden that air photographs had not detected it.

With daylight breaking, the 13th Battalion's tank caught up with the infantry and Harper ran out in front of it, beckoning it towards the trench. He was shot through chest and arm but his tank annihilated one gun and its crew. As in several instances, the other gun crew, shocked by the ease with which the tank had pulverised their comrades, surrendered. The stricken Harper (who survived) handed over to Lieutenant T. Dwyer, who completed the manoeuvre, and the second main obstacle had been overcome.

As expected, the defences in Hamel village itself and nearby Notamel Wood were strongest of all, and thirty tanks, including the three allotted to Pear Trench, had been instructed to support the infantry here. The 11th Brigade had the task of dealing with this part of the enemy front. The 43rd Battalion's objective was the village, while the 44th Battalion, split into two, moved past either side of the settlement, thus outflanking the central defences.

The Germans held Notamel Wood in strength and at first they did not feel particularly threatened because the approaching Diggers seemed to be uncertain where they were. Captain J. T. Moran, a Regular Army officer and at forty-four one of the oldest soldiers on the field, observed their hesitation and bellowed some parade-ground drill orders to put the men in the right direction. The orders were, 'Left incline!' followed by 'Right incline!'. The well-drilled men responded and were then heading directly for their objective.

Lieutenant L. S. Watts of the 43rd led his men in an encircling movement so that the enemy found themselves fired at from front and rear. But the Germans were expert in siting their defences so that every position was covered by one or more support machine-guns and two of these opened up on men of the 43rd and 44th, who had come together at this point.

A tank was hovering, waiting for opportunities. Watts' platoon sergeant ran up to it and, as instructed in training, yanked the pullrope of the back-door bell. When the officer looked out, the sergeant indicated the enemy gun position. An officer who witnessed the episode said, 'The tank went straight over to the problem and rubbed it out'.

The tanks overawed the German soldiers. The monsters advanced inexorably, no matter what was flung at them, and when they were close they fired point-blank into enemy positions with machine-guns and cannons, which fired grapeshot — steel balls similar to shrapnel but projected from a casing which burst. In confined spaces, the result was devastating. The heavy tanks flattened whole lines of trenches, weapon pits and shelters. The Germans had either to run or risk being crushed — and some did meet this dreadful end. Those who survived to surrender were shaking with fear and were more shocked than other Germans the Diggers had ever seen.

On the far northern flank, hard by the Somme River and its marshes, the company on the edge were affected by gas. It set them sneezing loudly enough for the Germans to hear, but the Diggers, still sneezing, cleared the Germans from the marshes.

At the other end of the Australian front, six-and-a-half kilometres to the south and moving east on the axis of the Roman road, the 6th Brigade had mixed fortunes. The 25th Battalion had the task of attacking the Germans at the very end of the German line to be assaulted. In this position they were inevitably going to be fired on from the flank, where the enemy was not under direct infantry attack.

The 25th and later the 27th were helped by the Australian Heavy Trench Mortar Battery, whose six mortars fired massive 9.45-inch shells which were lobbed into enemy positions in Monument Wood and on the railway line at Villers-Bretonneux.

Nevertheless, enemy machine-guns near the Roman road caused such heavy casualties among the two platoons that only nine men survived unwounded to charge and capture the enemy post. The 25th Battalion suffered ninety-three casualties, including two officers killed. The ninety-two German prisoners and nine machine-guns seized were hardly adequate compensation for the human loss.

The number of dead and wounded Australians might appear to indicate that the tanks were unhelpful, but those attached to the 6th Brigade were used so aggressively that they moved a full 1000 metres into enemy territory and demoralised the German resistance.

Individual initiative was evident everywhere, and not only in courageous attacks on enemy machine-guns. One of the most enterprising soldiers on that momentous day was Lance Corporal B. V. Schulz, of the 43rd Battalion, who had been assigned to search for enemy documents for analysis by Major Hunn and his intelligence staff. From a study of air photographs, Schulz had noticed faint signs of a buried cable leading first into Notamel Wood and then into the village itself. Schulz, with two German-speaking Americans as his mates, now tracked this cable, which led to an enemy dugout in the northern part of the ruined settlement.

On his instructions, the Americans called out to the occupants, advising them that they might as well surrender as they were surrounded. Actually, at that time they were *not* surrounded. Exploiting the fear in the voices of the enemy who responded, the American soldiers suggested that surrender was preferable to being killed underground by Australian grenades. The bluff worked. A German officer said they would surrender. The Americans warned him against any treachery, for if it occurred the attackers would show no mercy. There would be no tricks, the officer assured them. Lance Corporal Schulz, revolver drawn, then entered the dugout to receive the surrender of a battalion commander and his staff of about ten. There is no record of how the German officers felt about being forced to surrender to a Digger of lowly rank but it is easy to imagine their injured pride.

Another form of initiative was shown by Captain Moran when he took a bet that he would not dare put a French flag on the roof of a house. He would be a fine target for a sniper but Moran accepted the gamble and climbed out onto the rafters of a wrecked building and attached a flag to the highest point. An Australian photographer next day took shot of 'Moran's House' and it has been published in official histories.

Corporal T. Ryan of the 43rd Battalion was also enterprising. He had seen a dump of British ammunition, abandoned during the retreat following the German offensive in March. The dump was in a burning house set alight by Australian artillery early in the battle. At 9 am Ryan asked Lieutenant Canaway if he could salvage it, even though by now German guns were heavily shelling the village their infantry had lost. Given permission, Ryan took a party out under fire and brought back not only seventy-three boxes, each containing 1000 rounds of .303 rifle ammunition, but also cases of British grenades. Making several trips, he completed his volunteer mission without casualties to his party.

Another soldier prominent that day was Sergeant James Victor Lihou of the 13th Battalion. In charge of a Lewis-gun section, Lihou was in the leading wave of the attack and he advanced firing his gun from the hip. When he came upon an enemy post whose resistance threatened to stall the advance, he made a single-handed attack and so pre-occupied the crew that a bombing section approaching from the flank completed the destruction of the enemy post. Lihou, who had been awarded the Military Medal for his bravery at Hébuterne on 27 March, was decorated with the DCM for his work at Hamel.

Lihou was fatally wounded in an attack at Le Verguier two months later and I think it worth describing his exploit in this action as another example of courage and leadership which merited the award of the VC without its being given. With six men, Lihou had advanced ahead of his company and was cut off by an enemy machine-gun that opened fire to their rear. Lihou rushed the enemy post and threw a grenade that killed three of the crew. He took the survivors prisoner and advanced again with his party.

Meeting another nest of machine-guns he charged ahead, bombed and captured one crew and led his men into an enemy trench. Encountering an enemy post of twenty machine-gunners holding back another AIF battalion, Lihou climbed out of the trench alone to attack, but was wounded. He died on a stretcher on the way to a dressing station. Sergeant Lihou's body was lost during the fighting and his name in commemorated on the Villers-Bretonneux Memorial.

VCs were awarded for less than Lihou did on 18 September 1918. However, under the regulations, it was not possible to make a posthumous award other than a VC or a mere Mention in Despatches; nevertheless, Lihou was posthumously gazetted a second DCM. I speculate that perhaps the authorities who authorised decorations did not realise that he had died.

Most of the rank and file had only a vague idea of the extent of their attack. Signaller G. T. Gill of the 55th Battalion wrote in his diary on 4 July, 'There is going to be a big hopover in the morning ... Three or four divisions and some tanks are taking part'.

In fact, only 7500 men took part, drawn from battalions of five brigades. The full fighting strength of a division, with the 'left out of battle' men not included, was 12 000 men. Signaller Gill's estimate of the size of the attacking Australian force was greatly exaggerated.

During a battle, even an infantryman sees only that which is directly in front of him and which directly concerns him. Officers and some men, depending on their duties, might gain something of an idea of the progress of an operation, but other men further back can get quite the wrong impression. The only artillerymen who might have witnessed anything of the Hamel battle were the field gunners, but others were miles in the rear.

Similarly, while the foot soldiers would have received clear briefings from their platoon commanders, the gunners knew only that they were protecting their infantry by firing at invisible targets. The artillery officers and NCOs ordered the range and distance to be varied as the fire plan or an emergency dictated. Bombardier (artillery corporal equivalent) G. M. Rice kept one of the most detailed AIF diaries that have come to light, yet he did not know at the time that the operation of 4 July was an attack by his own Australian Corps. As his diary entry for 4 July makes clear, he believed that the Germans had attacked the Australians. Bombardier Rice wrote:

Weather fine and warm with fresh winds. Fritz was again shelling the position this morning with shrapnel and HE shells, which are known to us as 'woolly bears'. About 10 pm Fritz attacked on the divisional front and we received the SOS call immediately. Our guns were going in less than a minute and also the guns covering the whole of the sector. At the same time Fritz started on counter-battery work — that is shelling our batteries to stop or slow down our fire — and for about an hour he was sending them over 'thick and heavy'. We kept up our firing for about 2 hours during which time we had to wear our gas masks in the gun pits. One shell set fire to a farmhouse where some of us are billeted, also wounding one man. In addition a sergeant was gassed and had to be evacuated, but we all got our fair share of the fumes more or less. The whole stunt lasted about 2 hours but it was pretty hot while it did last. We hear that Fritz was knocked back everywhere and cut to pieces with barrage fire.

Confident in his planning for the battle and equally confident in his officers and men, Monash had allowed ninety minutes for the battle to be completed. He knew that there would be a counterattack and that the angry Germans would bombard the positions they had lost to the Australians, but all objectives would, he said, be taken by 4.40 am This was an audacious prediction. Not since the war began had any senior commander dared to put a time 'limit' on an operation. Some ventured an opinion that a battle could be over 'in days', and when it continued for months they looked ridiculous. A battalion commander would often order a patrol to be back in its own lines in one hour or two hours or before dawn. But to state in orders that an entire battle would be complete in one-and-a-half hours was, in the thinking of the time, absurd. Monash's calculations were just a little at fault — his battle lasted ninety-three minutes. He was not concerned about the extra three minutes. His troops had not let him down.

✦   ✦   ✦

Henry Dalzeil VC, a postscript

It is worth noting that Dalziel, known as 'Two Gun Harry', was the thousandth winner of the VC, which he received in the ballroom of Buckingham Palace on 13 December 1918. He saw action at Gallipoli, Mouquet Farm, Pozières, Guedeccourt, Lagnicourt, Bullecourt and Messines. He was said to have been wounded thirty two times during the war; on the last occasion his skull was smashed in and his brain exposed. Skilful medical treatment in Britain saved his life and he lived for another forty-seven years.

CHAPTER 8

The Feint Attack North of the Somme

History has largely ignored the feint or 'pretend' attack by the 15th Brigade, under Brigadier H. E. Elliott, north of the Somme River, yet the success at Hamel was partly due to the vigour of the 15th's work. The feint is acknowledged by plaques in the Australian Corps Memorial Park at Hamel, but it deserves even wider attention as it was a battle in itself.

Planned by Elliott, one of the great AIF leaders and prominent in April 1918 during the Battle of Villers-Bretonneux, Elliott divided his feint into several parts, a tactic designed to so occupy the Germans immediately north of the Somme that they could not transfer troops to what was bound to be an emergency at Hamel for the German High Command.

An ingenious 'attack' was made by only one officer and five of his men of the 55th Battalion. Men of the unit had made about twenty papier-mâché dummies which they clothed in Australian uniforms with rifles on their shoulders. Then, from the 55th's parapet on high ground at Sailly-Laurette, Lieutenant W. E. Campbell supervised the lowering and raising of these 'soldiers', so that the Germans opposite would see them and believe that the Australians were coming.

Altogether, had anybody counted, something like a hundred troops appeared to go over the parapet. Campbell timed this activity with the commencement of the Hamel attack at 3.10 am and he continued it for thirty-five minutes. German machine-guns fired thousands of rounds at the dummies, riddling them with bullets. Campbell and his men, safe in their trench, were amused and unharmed. The cost-effectiveness of this little manoeuvre was perfect.

Captain K. R. Wyllie's mission with 200 men was to raid German lines at a feature called Brick Beacon. They were provided with a barrage, including both medium and light trench mortars, but the guns had barely opened fire when the German artillery responded. The nervous rapidity of the enemy reaction was the result of the tension caused by the frequent Australian attacks during the previous weeks.

The men of the 55th Battalion were lying on their white-tape start line, with orders to stay there for three minutes and then advance as their own barrage moved forward. The German shells exploded among them, killing an officer and six men and wounding twenty-nine. Others were hit by machine-gun fire as they rushed towards the enemy trenches a hundred-metres distant. The raid had begun badly, but all the Germans in the first trench were killed except one sent back under guard for interrogation.

The second wave of attackers passed through the first, broke the enemy wire and rushed the second trench. Here Lieutenant L. N. Stafford killed two Germans but was himself shot dead. His mate, Lieutenant L. Chadwick, captured a machine-gun while his men blew up dugouts and a concrete platform on which a heavy machine-gun was mounted. (Lieutenant Stafford, aged twenty-nine, has no known grave and his name appears on the Australian National Memorial at Villers-Bretonneux.)

Good leading was needed because in the early morning gloom it was difficult for the men to keep direction. Having kept the Germans busy and, it was hoped, having convinced the German Command that Hamel was only part of the Australian objective, the raiders withdrew. The retirement was dangerous as a German barrage was now falling behind the men of the 55th. In attempting to pass through it to the safety of his own lines, Lieutenant W. T. Piddington was killed and some of the men were wounded. The Diggers took with them three prisoners and two light machine-guns were captured — at a cost of three Australian officers and sixty-four men hit. This part of the Hamel feint had been expensive but it was considered successful, and the officers were commended for their work. (Lieutenant Piddington is buried in Franvillers Communal Cemetery Extension, near Albert.)

Brigadier Elliott's third operation in making his feint was almost pre-ordained. He had earlier wanted to push forward his brigade's line east of Ville-sur-Ancre by making a night attack. It had been Elliott's brigade which had suffered so grievously in the British-planned assault at Fromelles, when the brigade was required to attack in sunlight. Ever since, Elliott had been cautious in his timing. His new line at Ville, if his brigade could succeed in establishing it, would be heavily shelled by enemy guns on Morlancourt Heights and he wanted his men under cover before daylight.

When Major General Joseph Hobbs, GOC 5th Division, was asked by Monash to provide the Hamel feint, he suggested to Elliott that the attack should be made by day. This idea was foolish and Elliott was forthright in rejecting it. He foresaw heavy loss among his men when the German artillery shelled them while they were digging in.

Now, as part of the Monash plan, a feint had to go in at 3.10 am, coinciding with the Hamel start. Elliott was satisfied with this because his men would be protected for a while by the gloom of very early morning and by a smokescreen. With Hobbs, he decided that this part of his feint would not be a raid like that at Brick Beacon, but that his troops would take and hold a length of new German trench.

His plans were ambitious. A single under-strength company, of only eighty men, would attack on a front of 700 metres, with the marshes of the River Ancre on their left. The area could then be held by scattered posts of experienced men. On the right of this company two companies of the 59th Battalion would capture 500 metres of German posts along a minor road. This part of Elliott's front also extended for 500 metres.

The tactics planned by the 58th and 59th companies were different one from the other and they show the thought now being applied by the AIF brigades entirely under Australian command. The 58th company commander, Captain F. C. Dawson, with an extended front, and a strength of only eighty men and limited manpower, used his soldiers in platoons (about twenty-five men at that time) and half platoons, each under a lieutenant or sergeant. Each had a particular objective, clearly defined through observation and on trench maps. The 59th Company's combat plan was for a line of scouts in pairs at the front, followed at ten metres distance by a line of small groups. After them, at twenty-five metres, were the Lewis gun sections, ready to fire ahead between the groups.

The Germans, though watchful, detected no sign of an attack; their usually thorough spotter planes had not noticed the artillery assembly. It was formidable for a short front, with all the 5th Division's guns, the mortars of three trench mortar batteries, guns from the Royal Horse

Artillery and with heavy guns supplied by British III Corps. When they all opened up at 3.10 am their fire was accurate and heavy.

As the shellfire lifted, the men of the right company under Captain G. W. Akeroyd rushed the German line with a great cheer, which may have been as demoralising as their fire because many of the defenders bolted through the crops. Within minutes, Lieutenant S. G. Facey blocked the right of the captured trench with two barricades so that he could not be attacked from the flank or enfiladed from there. This competent officer had won the DCM as a sergeant.

Some men of the other 59th company, which was led by Captain K. G. McDonald, ran into enemy wire cleverly placed in the concealing crops and were held up. On their right, Lieutenant W. J. McPherson jumped into the German trench just as an enemy machine-gunner opened fire from the parapet. When he was shot the trench was secured.

The centre platoons unfortunately lagged behind because of the wire and this gave German machine-gunners all the time they needed. They killed or disabled both platoon commanders, both sergeants and about half their men. Corporal A. Ibbotson survived this slaughter and located Captain McDonald, who sent him to bring all unwounded survivors on a roundabout route into McPherson's trench.

The setback was largely overcome by attacks along the German-held trenchline from left and right. Bombers of the 58th and 59th cleared the enemy block and linked up. Sentries shouted that German reinforcements were running forward and McDonald's Lewis gunners opened up on them at close range. When many of their number fell into the crops dead or dying, the others fled.

Meanwhile, Akeroyd's company was in trouble. As always, the Germans counterattacked, heavily grenading the length of trench captured by Lieutenant Facey over the barricades which his men were still strengthening. Facey was shot dead, and Captain Akeroyd and Lieutenant W. H. Scattergood were wounded. Pressure against the men holding the outer barricade was so great that the six men holding it ran back to the inner barricade. (Lieutenant Facey, aged, thirty-three, is buried in Méricourt-l'Abbé Communal Cemetery Extension, south-east of Albert.)

Lieutenant W. C. B. Stavely now commanded the company but he was not at the danger spot. However, an outstanding veteran NCO,

Sergeant P. L. Little, was there. He made his own way into the trench, ready to make himself useful. This was his chance. Taking charge, he found that the trench-block guard had too few bombs for a stiff fight and ordered the men back along the trench by fifty yards. Little knew that boxes of grenades were on their way and that he had to hold on until they arrived. The new company commander, Stavely, together with an Artillery forward-observation officer took charge of grenade collection, and Sergeant W. P. Hutchinson organised carrying parties. Through such teamwork, a notable feature of Australian battalions, Sergeant Little and the men he now commanded got their bombs and attacked. They not only retook the outer barricade but drove the Germans still further back with sniper fire. Little supervised the strengthening of the barricade and it remained in the Diggers' hands.

While Sergeant Little was dealing with a crisis on the far right of the line, on the left Captain Dawson was creating an unenviable 'record' in the AIF — with his eighty men he was attacking enemy posts on a greater length of line than had yet been attempted by the AIF in trench warfare — 750 yards (685 metres).

His operation started badly. Before zero, a reserve platoon under Lieutenant E. W. Tasker had been sent out to dig posts in the Ancre marshes, on the far left, ready to support Dawson if necessary. When he reached the stated position, Tasker met Lieutenant J. H. Fleming, in charge of the sector, who advised him that where he proposed to dig was much too boggy. 'I'll show you,' he said and led the way. In the gloom they passed an Australian listening post, whose men took them for enemy and threw a grenade. It wounded both officers. Tasker tried to continue, but realising that he was now unfit for command he telephoned his CO, who sent out Lieutenant W. Flintoft.

As the barrage lifted Dawson shouted to his small Company HQ staff, 'Come on, boys, they're off!'. Within seconds he was wounded as was Lieutenant J. E. Davies of the right platoon, but both continued in action. In the centre, Lieutenant H. D. Willis and his men killed two machine-gun crews. These losses may have had something to do with the rout of the numerous enemy opposing Willis. Captain Dawson, bleeding from facial wounds, arrived to find his right and centre secure but he had lost contact with the left.

Lieutenant I. G. Thompson, leading the left platoon of Captain Dawson's company, had been stopped by a machine-gun after only eighty metres. A vigorous, decisive officer, the twenty-one-year-old Thompson ordered his men to fan out and he led a charge on the post, killing the crews and capturing two machine-guns. Thompson's objective was a millhouse on the banks of the Ancre which was protected by wire entanglements and more machine-guns. His quick eye saw that he could attack from the flank, along the bank. Placing riflemen to fire at the gunners in and about the millhouse, he again led a charge, this time taking three more machine-guns and capturing the millhouse post.

Yet another Maxim opened up on Thompson's platoon and several men were hit. Thompson called on Corporal E. C. Skinner and some men to help him charge this post but he and Skinner were shot dead. Nevertheless, inspired by their young leader's courage and dash, the platoon's survivors held the objective.

Lieutenant Thompson's exploit was another one worthy of the VC. The supreme decoration may have been recommended but not approved. Had the VC not been the only decoration that could be awarded posthumously at that time, he would probably have been given the DSO or MC. However, his family had to be content with a simple Mention in Despatches. Lieutenant Thompson is buried in Ribemont Communal Cemetery Extension, south-west of Albert. Corporal Skinner has no known grave and his name appears on the Australian National Memorial at Villers-Bretonneux.

CSM A. E. McPhie had hurried to the flank on the Ancre to find out what had happened and, on his report, Dawson sent an order to Flintoft's reserve platoon to reinforce the mill-house position. In fact Flintoft, informed of the situation by a seriously wounded runner, Private L. A. Cook, had already advanced.

A gap remained on the left and this was filled by a platoon sent up by the 57th Battalion. With its arrival the new Australian front on this sector was complete. Brigadier Elliott had his new front line. Of course, it was shelled and the Germans were preparing an infantry counterattack but Captain McDonald, who observed the enemy assembly, fired a flare calling for an artillery barrage. It was so crushing that the German guns ceased firing after fifty minutes. The Australian and British guns continued for another half hour, by which time the Germans, steadily losing men, called off the counterattack.

The feint, then, was not wholly a feint but in part an actual attack. It achieved its two objectives — that of keeping most of the German reserves from being rushed to Hamel and of moving the Australian line forward in a key tactical area. It had cost the 15th Brigade the loss of fourteen officers and 128 men.

Brigadier Elliott keenly felt the loss of Lieutenant John Moore, killed by the German barrage. Moore was a fine officer with a splendid record. Aged twenty-nine, he had begun the war as a private soldier and had won the MM. Commissioned, he had twice been awarded the MC. Elliott specially transferred him from the 60th Battalion to trench mortars because of a crisis of morale among trench mortar soldiers. The Stokes mortars were issued with 'blue ring' bombs, which were notorious for the huge flash they caused when fired. This gave away the crew's position and attracted enemy artillery. Not long before Hamel, a bomb had burst prematurely, probably in the barrel, killing two of the crew and wounding another. Elliott, impressed by the respect of the men for Lieutenant Moore, asked him to transfer to Trench Mortars and renew the men's confidence in their weapon. He is buried in Méricourt-l'Abbé Communal Cemetery Extension, behind the Ville front.

The Germans were estimated to have had seventy-five killed or wounded; many fled, and sixty-four prisoners were taken. The Australians captured fifteen machine-guns. The result was considered excellent but the Australian losses prove that feints were not, as popularly believed, the 'easy' part of an operation.

I have long been worried about the injustice done to Lieutenant Thompson. He should have been awarded the VC.

CHAPTER 9

The German Counterattack

In most armies, infantry doctrine demanded that following an enemy assault there must be a counterattack, especially if valuable ground had been lost. And the counter had to be rapid, before the attacking force had time to consolidate. It was best to catch the enemy troops while they were still strengthening the defences on the ground they had occupied.

After heavy casualties it was not always possible for the British to launch a counterattack. The wounded had to be evacuated, units had to be reorganised and fresh junior leaders appointed to replace those who had become casualties. Tremendous will was necessary to make a counterattack, even with the help of reinforcement troops who had not suffered the trauma of a setback.

The Australians had learned from experience that the German Army went to extraordinary lengths to strike back fiercely and reoccupy positions lost. Therefore the AIF's doctrine was 'capture, consolidate, exploit'. Troops had a natural tendency after a successful attack to relax, sit down and smoke. Junior leaders — corporals, sergeants, lieutenants and captains — had to encourage and drive the men to dig in and prepare for the inevitable counterattack.

When reports of the Australian attack on Hamel reached the HQ of the German 43rd Reserve Division, which was responsible for that part of the front, there was at first only mild alarm. Over the previous few months the general and his staff had become resignedly accustomed to Australian raids. These were irritating and they unsettled the German troops, but obviously they were not intended to capture territory. Initially, therefore, the German Staff considered that the noise at Hamel might only be a raid in strength.

Nevertheless, a reserve battalion, the 1/202nd, stationed at Méricourt was ordered forward. This was a routine, methodical rather than an urgent movement. German military communications were good and it soon became clear that this suspected 'raid' extended from the Roman road at Villers-Bretonneux in the south all the way north to the Somme River, nearly 7000 metres. Added to this was a British artillery barrage north of the Somme and extending to the Morlancourt–Ancre River front.

As the hard-hitting and extensive nature of the Australian attack became evident the 43rd Division ordered the 201st Battalion, which was north of the Somme, to head for Hamel 'at once and rapidly'. Looking at their detailed wall map at HQ, the German Staff reckoned that the greater threat was south of the river. In any case, this was the most important sector, with a German salient protecting the positions on the heights east and south of Hamel village.

No doubt the officers and men of the German battalions were competent and willing but their progress was slow in the face of British air bombing and machine-gunning of moving troops.

The German leaders were not to know it, but the battle proper was over before the reinforcements reached their assembly points a mile east of the Wolfsberg. With the news that Hamel and the Wolfsberg had fallen, the Staff ordered the CO of the 1/202nd Battalion to 'retake these positions immediately'. Immediacy was out of the question and, after some false starts and further British air and artillery attack, just two companies detoured along the Somme valley to reach Accroche Wood. Australian artillery, operating on information from spotter planes, hindered German attempts to form up. Following orders from its Corps HQ, the German 43rd brought up yet another battalion as well as artillery. Theoretically, the force gathered for a counterattack was formidable, but all units were below strength.

AIF officers were not surprised when at 10 pm on 4 July the German artillery heavily bombarded the posts of the 11th Brigade on the line of the captured Wolfsberg.

The veterans knew that this pounding was the prelude to an infantry assault. It began with a party of bombers attacking up a long communication trench from a strong point which the enemy still held. Following the bombers came about 200 infantry. The local pressure was intense and at 10.10 pm an Australian 44th Battalion officer sent up a Very light signal, calling for his own guns to go into action. A British barrage began at once, crashing down on the German rear. This prevented reinforcements from moving but the attackers were well ahead of the bursting shells.

The Australian gunners could not drop shells on them for the very real fear that Australians would be hit. This reluctance to fire a barrage close to their own troops was greatly enhanced with the terrible reports that British and Australian guns had already killed many Australians with short-shooting during the advance. Gunners were always horrified by the results of their 'friendly fire'.

The counterattacking Germans knew the ground thoroughly and they quickly trapped twelve Diggers, most of them stretcher-bearers, in a deep dugout. The 44th Battalion men, running short of grenades despite the large quantity delivered by the tanks, fought furiously to hold back the determined Germans. A trench-mortar battery supported the Diggers by lobbing shells into the enemy communication trench to try to stop further reinforcement and resupply.

Soon the Germans held about 200 metres of trench, effectively dividing the southern and northern companies of the 44th. It was essential to stop this enemy success from spreading. Captain E. C. Adams called together some platoons and Lieutenants F. O. Gaze and C. R. Cornish organised a bombing attack from the southern direction while Captain W. J. Staples made a similar move from the north, the double-assault being co-ordinated through runners who skirted the area of fighting. The vital little operation could not take place until bombs had been brought up by carrying parties.

The night was wildly noisy and disturbed with the artillery of both sides firing and the Germans adding phosgene and mustard gas to their high explosive shells. The double assault began at 2 am but the experienced Germans were not taken by surprise and, by sustained fighting from behind trench-blocks, they stopped Captain Staples' drive.

From the opposite direction, Gaze and Cornish made good progress. According to the 44th Battalion history, the officers led their men in a 'bald-headed' attack, driving the Germans relentlessly from bay to bay. In the forefront of this spirited assault was Private J. J. Lynch, who in civil life, now well behind him, was an axeman. With a club and grenades, this powerful man kept the Germans retreating and actually got in among

Lieutenant General Sir John Monash, Commander of the Australian Corps. This photograph was taken at Villers Bretonneux on 25 May 1918 when Monash was a Major General; he was promoted to Lieutenant General soon after. (AWM E02350)

Wagons on a light railway deliver high explosive shells to gun positions.

An aerial photograph showing the results of intense shellfire on and around Hamel. The wavy lines at the bottom of the picture are the German trenches to the east of the village. (AWM 62d-P 1-10)

American troops near Corbie on 3 July 1918. They were on their way to join the Australians for the Battle of Hamel the following day. (AWM E2694)

Australian field-gunners in action in the summer of 1918. The gun is an 18-pounder.

The area in the centre of the battlefield over which the 4th Brigade advanced on 4 July. (AWM E02833B)

The famous German Pear Trench and the slope, at right, over which the Australians and supporting Americans advanced on 4 July. The enemy machine-guns in this forward position caused many Australian casualties, catching the Diggers against the breaking light. (AWM E02709)

The view from the observation post of the 13th Battalion near Vaire Wood, 3 July. All the white areas indicate digging or shellfire, with the chalk churned to the surface. The trees in the woods were generally devoid of foliage, which had been blasted away by shellfire. (AWM E2679)

Mark V tanks lurch through smoke towards the enemy line, early on 4 July.

Diggers and Doughboys dig in together during the Battle of Hamel. (AWM E02690)

Lieutenant General Sir John Monash, commander of the Australian Corps, presenting a decoration to a soldier of the AIF 2nd Division.

Private Henry Dalziel wearing the Victoria Cross, his award for great gallantry during the battle. (AWM A5444)

Diggers in a position which a few hours before had been occupied by the Germans. Wrecked Hamel lies behind them. (AWM E02844A)

Exhausted stretcher-bearers resting by a track along which wounded were carried from Hamel to a motor-loading point in Hamelet. Notice the men's 'SB' brassards and their stretchers. (AWM E02701)

One of the few tank casualties of the Hamel operation, a Mark V lies crippled in the village. Captain Moran's flag flutters from a wrecked house. (AWM E03843)

The Australian Corps Memorial at Le Hamel, France. (John Laffin)

The modern village of Le Hamel. In the foreground a few of the 22 plaques which describe the course of the battle. They are situated on the site of the German position known as Wolfsberg. (John Laffin)

them, creating havoc until he was shot in the head. Lynch's name is commemorated on the Villers-Bretonneux Memorial.

The enemy broke and ran from the main trench into the communication trench, frantically heading for their own lines. Many fell to the Diggers' grenades, snapshots and to Lewis gun fire. At no point did the Germans look like making a stand. They were driven out of the communication trench and from a section of fighting trench which they had continued to hold after the original Australian attack in the morning. Separately, in the northern length of trench and in the southern section, enemy troops were bottled up in dugouts, from which six German officers and fifty other ranks were captured, together with ten machine-guns. The twelve Diggers, taken by the Germans at the beginning of their counterattack, were freed.

For the Germans, the counterattack was a complete disaster. The Diggers' riposte was classic in its execution and it put the seal on the entire Hamel operation.

The German hold on Villers-Bretonneux Ridge was greatly weakened as a result of the battle and, even more importantly, the British position was strengthened. German losses in men and materiel were significant. About 2000 Germans were killed; forty-three officers and 1562 other ranks were captured. The Australians seized two new model anti-tank machine-guns, 177 Maxim medium machine-guns, thirty-two trench mortars and a new anti-tank weapon, a huge rifle weighing 16½ kilograms which was mounted on a bipod and fired a round of .530-inch calibre. It was ineffective during the battle.

Brigadier E. A. Wisdom, GOC AIF 7th Brigade, reporting on the battle, claimed that an English-speaking prisoner told his captors: 'You bloody Australians — when you are in the line you keep us on pins and needles. We never know when you are coming over'. This sounds embarrassingly like a fabricated quotation and something the Australians would *like* to have heard from the lips of a German.

However, the sentiments were true enough. Because of the Diggers' 'peaceful penetration' the Germans opposite them lived with the strain of anticipation. North of the Somme from April onwards they had been in a constant state of apprehension because of Australian raids and what can be classed as 'minor' battles, such as that at Ville-sur-Ancre in May and Morlancourt in June. Hamel was the most damaging of a series of blows to the Germans.

A German official history gives information about the counterattack on Brigadier Elliott's Ville-sur-Ancre front. A 'deliberate' counterattack after an artillery barrage was ordered for 8.30 pm. The attack was to be made by a battalion of the 54th Reserve Division of Württembergers, which had been in Dernancourt, south of Albert. The Württembergers' historian makes the honest comment, 'We knew that the 247th was not in a condition to retake a lost trench'. He also states: 'When our artillery opened, the English [sic] immediately replied with the strongest barrage and the counterattack could not be carried out'.

The best the local German Command could do, the historian admits, was to re-organise the companies, which had been thrown into disarray by the 15th Brigade's attack, and to hold their former support line as their new front.

The German histories, which are generally objective, comment on the speed of the Australians' attack at Hamel and on the 'fierce and determined nature' of their response to the German counterattack.

They may have been surprised too by the Australian raids that followed that very night of 4–5 July. At 3 am, when the German defenders were most likely to be exhausted from the exertions of the previous twenty-four hours, a fighting patrol of the 13th Battalion raided an enemy post on the right of the line, killed some enemy and brought in three prisoners. Australian artillery also harassed the Germans throughout that night.

Had the German Command counterattacked in the early hours of 5 July they would have faced fresh Australian units. Still going by the Monash plan, the 49th Battalion relieved the hard-hit 15th Battalion on the left sector from Huns Walk to the Brigade boundary and the 39th Battalion replaced other weary Diggers. Monash seems to have left nothing to chance. He had wrested the initiative from the Germans and he intended to keep it.

As with other setbacks, the German Command studied the reasons for the Hamel defeat. The senior staff concluded that the main weakness had been 'the absence of a forward defensive position, so allowing the British tanks to effect penetration'. By this they meant a stronger line than that which included Pear Trench forward of Hamel itself and the positions on the Wolfsberg ridge, and in Vaire, Hamel and Accroche Woods. By German thinking, a strong position across the flat fields, with anti-tank ditches, broad bands of barbed wire and blockhouses, would have stopped the tanks, thus depriving the Australian infantry of their protection. This may have been so as, once they had fallen into a well-constructed ditch, the tanks of the period could not climb out.

The German study also conceded that British aerial bombing had weakened their reserves and preventing their effectively forming up. It must always be remembered that the RAF's invaluable contribution to the Hamel success had been requested and outlined by Monash as part of his all-arms plan.

While the German Staff did not blame the German infantry in the analysis, many troops had surrendered with unusual rapidity — not that this was admitted in the report.

Brigadier E. A. Wisdom gave his opinion that the German generals were holding the Hamel line with their poorest troops. He may have had reason to believe this at the time but later studies show that this was not so. Wisdom was being unfair to the German enemy in the line at Hamel, and even more so to his own men, who had outfought the Germans. Regardless of the quality of the infantry, the machine-gunners were definitely not poor troops. It was these élite soldiers, superior in quality to almost any other formations on either side during the war, who inflicted the greatest casualties on the Australian attackers at Hamel.

Some soldiers saw many German prisoners and would not have agreed with Brigadier Wisdom's assessment of their quality. For instance, Sergeant Bruce Rainsford of the Army Medical Corps was at the front when prisoners were being brought in. In a diary entry of 4 July he states: 'Prisoners were well equipped, in good condition and of a very good type'.

The HQ of German XI Corps sent a special inquiry to the commander of the German 43rd Reserve Division and it may have similarly dealt with the 13th Division. Corps wanted an explanation for the reverse. The divisional general and his staff replied that there was no need for an investigation to fix the blame on any troops or individual commander of any rank. This curt response was defensive but it was also honest. The German leaders responsible for the Hamel–Ville line had been out-thought and outfought by superior generalship and soldierly skill. Naturally, they could not put that in writing.

The German Staff may have been surprised by the depth of knowledge about their units possessed by Australian (and British) intelligence. The AIF 4th Division issued several reports to officers of all fighting units on the Hamel line to inform them of the 'combat status' of German units. They were marked CONFIDENTIAL and were not for general distribution to all ranks in case soldiers were taken prisoner and disclosed that their own officers were well informed about the enemy.

An 'Intel Summary' of 3 July told officers exactly what enemy units would be facing them. The 13th Division would be in the central sector, with the 13th Regiment in North Vaire Wood, the 35th Regiment in a defined area of the wood, the 15th Regiment in South Vaire Wood, the 13th Company and the 58th Regiment in the Vaire Wood Sector. The summary goes on to give an assessment of the 13th Division:

The 13th relieved the 77th Res. Div. about 1 July. It is a division of good quality. During 1915 the Westphalians distinguished themselves by excellent work on defences and fought tenaciously on all occasions. At Verdun and on the Somme, too, the 77th acquitted itself well. Both in 1916 and 1917 however, desertions were not infrequent, these being mostly on the part of Poles and Alsatians, who are found in large numbers in the division. The division received a smashing blow on the Ailette in October 1917 [from the French] and the drafts required to bring it up to strength again have not yet been put to the test. It is therefore not possible to estimate the value of the division at the moment.

The division's 'value' became clear twenty-four hours later. It fought stubbornly.

CHAPTER 10

High Spirits; Sad Episodes

The attitude of the Diggers who took part in the battle of Hamel was significantly different from that in earlier battles. They had gone into it rested, fed and confident. While they did not know all the details of the planning by Monash, Sinclair-MacLagan and their staffs, it was clear to the men that this show was 'different'. They had been given a fighting chance, something that had been grimly lacking in major operations under British command. Before the earlier battles there had been talk such as, 'This is going to be another bloody stunt' and, 'We'll never get the Huns out of their dugouts' and, 'Get ready for a long, hard slog'.

Before Hamel, every man knew that the 'the Heads' — as they called the senior officers — expected the stunt to be over in one day. According to C. E. W. Bean, the attitude of the men throughout the fight was 'noticeably carefree'. No soldier going into a fight against the Germans was ever carefree and most of the men at Hamel soon saw mates killed or wounded, which was always a depressing experience. Bean's description of the Diggers' 'carefree' manner may have been influenced by comments from some of the officers. For instance, Lieutenant Harry Conrad of the 42nd Battalion noted that 'Numbers 14 and 15 platoons hopped joyfully over'. Getting into action was a relief after a build-up of tension. A month later, on the first day of the great Allied offensive, Lieutenant Conrad was killed at the age of thirty-two. He is buried in Heath Cemetery, Harbonnières, Somme.

At Hamel there was certainly something devil-may-care about the Diggers, some of whom passed through their own barrage, a desperately dangerous action, to hunt for prisoners and trophies. Incorrigible souvenir-hunters, the Diggers had been risking their lives for trophies throughout the war. The pickings were good at Hamel because there were so many prisoners and because the Germans, in their haste to withdraw, left much property in dugouts, trenches and the ruins of the village.

Platoon officers reported interesting, Digger-like exchanges, most of which occurred once the immediate danger had passed. As men of the 14th Battalion were digging a trench, Lieutenant J. D. Craven heard one soldier say to his mate, 'Do you think Fitzroy'll beat Carlton on Saturday?' The 14th was a Victorian battalion.

Men of the 43rd were in front of Notamel Wood, on the left flank, waiting for the next move, when Lieutenant T. W. B. Roberts heard, 'What'd you do, Bill, if you were pinned down by the feet by a tank and a box of ammunition was falling on your head from an aeroplane?' Clearly, the new experience of operating with tanks and planes was having its effect.

A surprising number of Diggers kept diaries, although officially they were forbidden, and several of them commented on the Hamel battle.

Private F. E. Brewer of the 20th Battalion, which was on the right of the Australian line, wrote colourfully about the battle's commencement and with satisfaction about its progress:

Roar terrific. The whole line in front of us is ablaze with flashes leaping up and convulsing like the fiery fingers of ten thousand devils tearing at the sky. Latest news 'All well'. The 6th Brigade [Brewer's own Brigade was the 5th] going strong. Success of stunt evident everywhere. Columns of prisoners are now coming down the roads and the tanks are coming back, the cheerful crews sitting on top of them. Jerry has come another gutzer so the boys say.

The tanks left the battlefield at 5.30 am, so Brewer was writing in his diary before 6 am that 4 July.

But amid the lightheartedness, high spirits and excitement there was much sad sentiment. Every soldier's death was a tragedy, affecting his mates and comrades and later his family when the dreaded news reached them. At Hamel, several distressing incidents occurred, such as the burial of three Diggers in the one grave. Those interred were Captain Fred Woods, Lieutenant H. E. Blee and CSM Harold Blinman of the 16th Battalion. All three had been sergeant-major of the same company and they were mates. They stayed together in death for a time, though later, in 'regular' burials, they were given individual graves. All three are officially listed as having died of wounds but they did not live long enough for stretcher-bearers to carry them off the battlefield. They are buried in Daours Communal Cemetery Extension, east of Amiens, where are buried men of more different AIF units than anywhere else on the Western Front.

Among the Australian dead was cheerful twenty-year-old Private Thomas Parrish of the 13th Battalion. A bright and alert soldier, he had been given the task of guiding a tank from its conning tower. He was killed while carrying out this task. His elder brother Joseph, aged twenty-one, of the 4th Battalion Australian Machine Gun Corps, had died of wounds in a base hospital the previous week, 27 June 1918. The brothers had been born in Wales and had emigrated to Australia with their parents, who lived at Teralba, NSW. Joseph (snr) and Martha Parrish had not wanted their boys to grow up in the squalid dangers of a Welsh colliery. Such a life would have been less dangerous than as front-line soldiers in the AIF.

Tom Parrish has no known grave. He would have been buried, but perhaps his identity discs were lost and, when he was disinterred for formal burial, nobody knew who he was. His headstone would carry the inscription 'Unknown Australian Soldier of the Great War'. His name is engraved on the Villers-Bretonneux Australian National Memorial, together with the names of 13 000 other Australians who have no known grave in France. Joseph Parrish is buried in Terlicthun British Cemetery, Wimille, Pas de Calais.

The end of Lieutenant Ramsay Wood of the 14th Battalion was an especially tragic one. Wood, aged thirty-one, had already established himself in civil life as a journalist in Melbourne. Well known in the 14th Battalion, Wood and Lieutenant E. J. Rule were dealing with part of Huns Walk when a white flag was waved above a parapet. Rule and Wood, with four men, walked over to take prisoner the surrendering enemy. As they approached they were again fired on and a tank came up to accompany the little party. While this was happening a shellburst from the Australian barrage killed Rule's batman, Private D. W. Floyd, and Corporal H. S. Cochrane was then shot through the head. Germans ran from the approach of the tank and the two officers jumped into the trench and followed them. They had bolted into two dugouts and Rule, angry at the firing which followed the surrender, shouted in German to the enemy to come out. The Australian officers were ready to kill but, to their astonishment, there emerged what Rule called 'a crowd of young boys'. 'With a boot to help them along they ran with their hands over their heads back to our lines,' Rule wrote.

Wood and Rule stood and looked along the trench for further enemy movement, either in surrender or rapid retreat. At this point Wood was shot through the head by a German whom Rule could not see. To hold the key trench position, Rule brought up a section of men and some Lewis gunners, for the position blocked the retreat of the enemy at this part of the front. Small groups of Germans, who realised that they were trapped, turned up to surrender later in the day. Rule, who had seen many Australians killed, was upset by the death of his mate, Ramsay Wood. Lieutenant Wood is buried in Crucifix Corner Cemetery, Villers-Bretonneux.

Two aircraft were lost during the battle, one being shot down by an enemy fighter. The end of the other was more problematic. Also, it was dramatic and tragic. The observer in the plane was seen to throw out his box of ammunition attached to a parachute, which became hooked on a wing. Enthralled infantrymen on the ground watched as the pilot struggled to steady his plane and then, having handed over the dual-control machine to his observer, he bravely climbed out onto the wing to clear the parachute and its dangling box of ammunition. By the time he had done so the plane had descended from 1200 feet to about one hundred feet and the pilot was again at the controls. For some seconds the attention of the soldiers was more on the drama above them than on their targets. Then the plane went into a dive, possibly after being hit by a shell, and crashed. Troops who rushed to help found the pilot dead and the observer dying.

After the battle the French prime minister Georges Clemenceau visited the Australians at Bussy and spoke to them in English. Major General Sinclair-MacLagan led the Diggers in three cheers for the prime Minister. The impression given by official histories is that the Diggers were in a euphoric state on this occasion, but comments in the diary of Major Burford Sampson of the 15th Battalion shows — probably for the first time in print — the reality of this stage-managed occasion.

On 7 July, while in Pioneer Switch Trench at Hamel, Sampson wrote:

CO to Brigade HQ, then to Bussy to meet French President. Twenty-five men from each battalion who were in the stunt. [That is, each battalion was required to select a small number to attend the celebratory occasion.] A damn shame to drag tired and strained men from the line. As usual, all the wasters on Div HQ, A.P.Ms & M.P.s in the foreground [Assistant Provost Marshals and Military Police]. The real Billjim [the dinkum Digger] not given a chance. Recommendations being sent in. Difficult to get the stories out of the men & find the right man. Capt Glasgow [DSO, MC] showed out above the others when the line was held up at Pear Trench.

The next day Sampson again wrote with exasperation, indignation and cynicism: 'Men just played out physically and mentally. God help us if the Hun attacks with weight. What a beauty our English GOC is, goes on leave with his division still in the line after doing a fine stunt. No thanks to his rotten staff anyway. Wind vertical [A cogent way of saying that the staff had the 'wind up']'.

Earlier, on 5 July, Sampson noted that his battalion HQ had received a screed concerning honours and awards. The battalion was notified that it could nominate two officers and thirty men. 'What an insult!' Sampson wrote. Knowing how many officers and soldiers had distinguished themselves, Sampson was angry at the limitation of awards. Even more infuriating was the fact that this limitation was being imposed by staff officers who would see to it that they received decorations through reciprocal recommendation among themselves.

Sampson assumed command of the 15th Battalion on 6 August when his CO, Lieutenant Colonel Terence McSharry, was killed close to the battlefield where he and his unit had so distinguished themselves. A Queenslander, McSharry, aged thirty-five, was a Gallipoli veteran and had proved himself to be one of the best battalion commanders of the war. His unit was in bivouac on the Somme flats at Vaire ready for its march to assembly points on the night of 7 August, before the great offensive of the 8th. A German artillery barrage hit the 15th and caused casualties. McSharry was helping a wounded man into shelter when a shell exploded, killing him, his adjutant and the intelligence officer; forty others were killed or wounded. Three AIF generals and many battalion commanders were present at McSharry's burial, in Corbie Communal Cemetery Extension, Somme. He was one of the AIF's most decorated soldiers — CMG, DSO and Bar, MC.

CHAPTER 11

The Wounded; The Tanks; The Americans; Aeroplanes

Certain features of the Battle of Hamel must be singled out for special attention, partly for their intrinsic interest and also because they were unique, or different from earlier battles.

For instance, while tanks had been employed at Flers in 1916 (wastefully and fruitlessly), at Bullecourt in 1917 (disastrously), and at Cambrai in 1917 (successfully but in the end without advantage), at Hamel they were used in an innovative and enterprising way with complete success.

Clearing of the wounded from the battlefield had been thought out and was effected with more celerity than in any other battle or segment of a larger battle to that time.

Aircraft had been in the skies above the fighting since 1914. At Hamel the new air arm was used in a much more co-ordinated way than in any other operation not just to that time but for the entire war. It also had more functions than ever before.

American soldiers had been in the Western Front theatre of war for some months and were training with the British Empire armies and with the French, but at Hamel they took part in their first battle. Their behaviour, and comments about them as soldiers by the veteran Australians, are among the most interesting aspects of a fascinating battle.

Added to all this was the difference in the Australians themselves. The officers had never before seen the Diggers in such a buoyant mood.

The Wounded

The men of the Australian Army Medical Corps were among the first to know of an impending attack by their infantry. Private H. E. Gussing, of 1st Field Ambulance, and in civil life a chemist from Ashfield, NSW, noted in his diary on 3 July: 'We issued shell dressings [bandages] to the 14th Brigade, so 'tis dinkum about the stunt. It has been advertised as a demonstration only but they are generally costly. We have made every preparation possible — extra men & cars and dressings sent forward'.

Gussing was one of many cynics who had learned from experience that when the 'Heads' announced that a stunt was merely to be a 'demonstration' — meaning a show of force — casualties were likely to be heavy. He was to discover that Hamel was no mere demonstration but an attack in strength, as his entry for 4 July showed:

Am Day of Indep. & 'tis being celebrated everywhere as a compliment to the Yanks. At 3.10 am the guns opened up right along our front and instantly flares of all kinds were sent up by Fritz. It was a great sight. We are high up & can see the line of flashes of the guns & the flares making the night bright. Towards 6 am the cases started to arrive & for a time we were very busy. I took all the walking wounded cases giving them all A.T. [anti-tetanus injections]. Eased off at 10 am & I had breakfast. Our sector was one of the easiest, about 200 cases.

Gussing's cases were bullet wounds, some of them multiple; others came from shrapnel and shell shards, a few from grenade fragments.

As Private Gussing implies in his diary entries, as much thought had been given to clearing the wounded from the battlefield as to the attack against the enemy. Walking wounded were able to get themselves to their own RAP and from there they were directed or helped to main dressing stations, field ambulances or casualty clearing stations. Stretcher-bearers carried back many wounded to the same pre-arranged posts. All finished up at one or other of the three motor-loading points.

It had been foreseen that tanks returning from the fighting would be able to help in the evacuation of the wounded. They brought back many soldiers, either on top of the tank or inside, but the regimental medical staff and the tank crews had been ordered not to carry men with abdominal wounds or fractures.

Gathering in the wounded was unexpectedly rapid and at the motor-loading points not enough ambulances were ready, so that at times up to eighty wounded were awaiting transportation. The chief medical officer of the 4th Division sent a staff officer to take charge and he at once ordered more cars and all horse-drawn ambulances to the spot. By noon all the wounded — every man had already received primary care — were being treated in hospitals.

One of the best descriptions of removal of wounded was given in a report by Lieutenant Frank E. Schram, US Medical Corps, attached to the AIF 15th Battalion.

We moved from Brigade HQ to Battalion HQ at 10.30 pm, accompanied by 5 hospital men [medical orderlies] and 2 stretcher-bearing squads (16 men) taken from Field Hospital. Those Field Hospital stretcher-bearers were taken with us so that on their return they could let Field Hospital know where our RAP was.

We moved from Battalion HQ about 12.45 am, accompanied by these men, to No-Man's-Land. It had been previously arranged with Colonel McSharry to do a 'hop-over' with the troops, as there was no suitable RAP in their present trenches without the carrying distance being too great, the idea being to establish ourselves in an RAP in the new trenches.

We lay in No-Man's-Land until the barrage started, then moved forward with the troops. We attended wounded men in No-Man's-Land while the barrage was going on.

We reached pear-shaped trench with the troops, looked for a suitable dugout and could find none, so we did our dressings in the open trench. Cases were brought in rather fast but we dressed and got them out in rapid time. The carrying distance from our RAP to the ADS was approximately a mile. To start with there was no relay post established but after a few trips a relay post was set up midway between the RAP and ADS.

We had some difficulty in getting rid of our dress cases. [Seriously wounded who needed specialist attention.] They were not evacuated fast enough. We had difficulty for a while in obtaining sufficient stretchers. Our supply of Thomas splints [for broken limbs] ran out and could not be replenished for a time. As a consequence we had to use rifles as splints. Of all the cases that I saw and dressed no tourniquet was used. Pressure with the shell dressings was sufficient to check the haemorrhages.

We had 12 stretcher-bearers from each company [in addition to the original 16], also one man in charge of each stretcher-bearing detail from the company, which made 3 stretcher-bearing squads. Four Americans were assigned to each bearing section and these were mixed or distributed with experienced Australians, so that each stretcher squad had at least one American and experienced Australians.

It was impossible to use diagnosis tags on each case because they came in too fast and to use diagnosis tags would delay the wounded in getting out.

I recommend that our present First-aid packet be replaced by a larger sized dressing, similar to that used by the Australians; that heavy scissors be supplied one to each bearer squad and one to each MO; that an ample supply of Thomas splints, elbow splints and plain board splints be supplied. That cotton or wool be provided in ample quantities and also bandages; that morphine be furnished by the Field Hospital.

All recommendations made by Schram were adopted, bringing the US Army Medical Service in the field up to the standard of the AIF. Schram was awarded the British decoration, the MC, for his work during the battle.

It is all too easy for accounts of 'a glorious, successful and rapid victory at low cost' to give the impression that nobody involved suffered very much. Statistics of casualties are so neat and ordered that many people see them merely as another kind of balance sheet. The only men who saw behind the bland words and the simple figures were the Diggers on the spot — and the nurses who cared for the wounded and helped the seriously hurt to die with dignity.

Relatively few of these front-line soldiers and their nurses have left a frank and honest account of the horrors of war, perhaps because they did not want to stir memories that were better left uncovered, and certainly very often to spare their families from the ghastliness of the truth.

One of the best Digger witnesses of the war was Private F. J. Brewer of the 20th Battalion, 5th Brigade, 2nd Division, who kept a detailed diary which spares neither himself nor its readers any horror. Shortly before Hamel he wrote:

This was my first night under regular gunfire. My feelings were those of curiosity and fear, but I was calm and master of myself and, like most other men, did not allow myself to degenerate into what the boys, in their forcible language, call 'a windy bastard'.

The whole line in this sector was lighted like George Street, Sydney, on a Friday night, and gave me the impression that the Huns were very nervous.

INFANTRY CASUALTIES

4th Brigade	Officers	OR
13 Bn	8	118
14 Bn	2	53
15 Bn	9	231
16 Bn	5	73
4 TM Battery	--	5
Total	24	480

11th Brigade	Officers	OR
41 Bn	--	7
42 Bn	3	48
43 Bn	7	90
44 Bn	5	149
11 TM Battery	--	2
Total	16	296

6th Brigade	Officers	OR
21 Bn	--	52
23 Bn	3	70
6 TM Battery	--	1
Total	3	123

7th Brigade	Officers	OR
25 Bn	3	90
Others	2	20
Total	5	110

15th Brigade	Officers	OR
57 Bn	1	10
58 Bn	2	39
59 Bn	6	58
60 Bn	3	20
15 TM Battery	2	1
Total	14	128

33rd American Division

According to Bean, the Americans had 175 casualties in all. American figures mention 114 and 121. The two sources also disagree about the number of killed — thirteen and twenty-six. No American officers were reported killed.

Describing digging a trench under fire, Brewer notes:

Here I was introduced to 'whizzbangs', which burst about us at intervals; 'pineapple bombs' that spat tails of fire in their wake; and 'coal boxes', missiles that burst with a high explosive effect...

For two long hours, which seemed years ... an inferno shook as in the throes of an earthquake. The grunting of the German batteries became more frequent and vigorous ... several men, in a state of panic, rushed from their dugouts. They were quickly wounded. Stretcher-bearers came forward calmly through the storm and bore the wounded away to the Regimental Aid Post.

Explicitly Brewer describes a sergeant being cut in two by a huge shell splinter — which I too am reluctant to publish — and goes on: 'Another NCO some minutes later was mortally wounded together with several privates. So pleased were some of the wounded to have 'got a blighty' that they could be seen laughing on the stretchers as they were being carried away'.

Not long before Hamel, one of Brewer's diary entries reads:

Ghastly sight encountered at crossroads where a heavy shell had fallen, killing or wounding sixty men who had been sleeping in adjacent houses. On one side of the road the dead were piled up in a bloody mass, flesh, blood and khaki being rolled into a pulp. Limbs were mangled, heads broken open and faces compressed and resembling pieces of crumpled blood-stained paper. Heaps of timber, plaster and bricks blocked up the roadway. We went on our way in a mood of indescribable wretchedness.

Having described the death of comrades killed by shells while asleep, Brewer notes, 'I am now well used to the blood and slaughter but the death of comrades affects one terribly'.

Shortly before the Hamel fighting, Private Brewer also wrote:

At dusk some American troops marched into the wood to bivouac for the night. This was their first acquaintance with actual warfare. All appeared to be terrified of gas. Shells whistling over in their natural flight naturally made them very nervous and they asked repeatedly, 'Is that gas?' Apparently the Yanks had been marching for days as they complained of having sore feet and asked eagerly for water.

Sore feet and thirst — soldiers are always thirsty before and during a battle — were minor worries. The victory at Hamel might have been achieved with fewer casualties than usual on the Western Front but the statistics indicate serious enemy resistance.

It is not possible to arrive at a figure for casualties caused by 'friendly fire'. From incidental references in the official histories, battalion histories and soldiers' letters and diaries I estimate that up to 20 per cent of casualties may have been caused in this way, but I stress that this is only a personal unofficial estimate. Major Burford Sampson states in his diary: 'Many of our men killed by short shooting of the barrage'. He was referring to the fight at Pear Trench.

Signaller G. T. Gill of the 55th Battalion, which was in action north of the Somme River in the so-called feint attack, contributes similar evidence. In his diary entry of 4 July he wrote: '55th 2Co [two companies] only went over — had good many casualties — own mortar'. Brief though this is, it is important; the infantry's own mortar bombs were exploding among them.

The subject of 'own casualties' was distasteful to C. E. W. Bean and though he mentioned several incidents in passing he did not stress them and nowhere does he refer to any incompetence or carelessness. He would not have wanted to cause further distress to the men's families, many of whom would have still been alive when his volume of the *Official History* in which Hamel is described, was published in 1942.

Probably he would have thought of them as accidents of war. As every front-line soldier and the army medical services know, such tragedies are common during fighting. There are authenticated stories of nervous sentries shooting their own men in the dark as they approached their trenches after a patrol. A saying common among soldiers on sentry duty in an isolated outpost was, 'Shoot first, ask questions later'.

Some such incidents occurred when men approaching their own lines in the dark, mist or battle smoke did not hear the challenge, 'Who goes there?' Perhaps, too, they had forgotten the password. Many a sentry, tense, tired and fearful for his own life would open fire in suspicious circumstances. On one occasion at Fromelles a sentry killed two of his mates — they were one behind the other — with a single shot. I am sure that my estimate of 20 per cent 'own casualties' is not an exaggeration.

The Tanks

None of the dominion armies possessed any tanks of their own and no Australian troops had taken part in the Battle of Cambrai, in November 1917, when the Tank Corps had been the deciding factor in the British victory.

History seems to be only dimly aware that some Diggers had seen something of tank warfare more than two months before Hamel. At Villers-Bretonneux on 24 Aril 1918, thirteen German tanks, mostly A7Vs, engaged British and Australian infantry. British Mark IVs took on three A7Vs and drove them off. Soon after this historic first tank-versus-tank engagement an Australian pilot called up seven British light Whippet tanks to charge German infantry.

News of the Villers-Bretonneux episode seems not to have reached the AIF rank and file or even the officers. Everything that the AIF thought it knew about the tanks was bad. They had been assured at Bullecourt in April and May 1917 that they could depend on the tanks. But the tanks failed lamentably and tragically and the Diggers considered them useless. Indeed, they hated them.

Monash had not been present at Bullecourt, but even if he had been it is certain that he would still have seen their potential. He did not at first manage to impart his confidence in them to Sinclair-MacLagan, GOC 4th Division, who would be in charge of the Hamel operation.

Rawlinson, Monash's superior, agreed with his suggestion to use tanks and he went further: The attack must be made with a number of tanks sufficient to ensure success. This general, who had presided over the colossal disaster of the Battle of the Somme, was now conscious of the need to keep Australian casualties to a minimum; hence his support for the tanks. However, he understood Sinclair-MacLagan's reluctance and noted in his diary: 'MacLagan [sic] is not overjoyed at the prospect of tanks but we will get him round when he has had experience of the new type'.

As I have described in Chapter 6, the officers and men of the Tank Corps went to great lengths to 'get the Australians round'.

Rawlinson may have been favourably influenced about tanks following a protest by Brigadier Hugh Elles, GOC of the Tank Corps, that tanks were being ignored. Like Brudenell White, Elles had the courage and confidence to stand up for his new arm and was bold enough to criticise GHQ and therefore Haig himself. GHQ anticipated a German offensive and had issued a paper entitled 'Memorandum on Defensive Measures', which Elles had read. He was alarmed to find little references to tanks.

In his protest to GHQ, Elles said there was a need 'to think ahead in order to take advantage of an arm which at present the enemy is not fully prepared to counter. The eventual counter to the tank can only be the tank. We have an opportunity. Once tank meets tank the opportunity will be lost'. He pressed this point by urging GHQ to create new tactics to take advantage of the arrival of the new Mark V tank. Tank tactics, he further stated, must be offensive. No wonder, then, that the GHQ memo stressing defensive measures so worried him.

Conscious that infantry commanders were ignorant of the tank's role, on 27 June Tank Corps HQ distributed an educational paper which noted that:

The effect of tanks leading forward infantry may be compared to that of the artillery barrage but the infantry should not look on it as such, but should regard the tanks as armoured fighting patrols or mechanical scouts, thrown forward not to exonerate them from fighting but to give them more latitude in the use of their machine-guns, rifles and bayonets.

In elaboration, the tanks were to capture ground; the infantry was to help them in overcoming strong points, to mop-up trenches and consolidate the position. Mopping-up was the term used to describe eliminating pockets of resistance.

At Hamel, tank-infantry co-operation did not work out quite like this, as the description of the battle shows, but the Mark V was infinitely more attractive to the Diggers than the earlier model employed at Bullecourt in April–May 1917. To say that the Australian troops were spellbound and full of admiration for what the tanks could do is not to overstate their attitude.

The Diggers had good reason to be intrigued by tanks, once they had overcome the prejudice against them produced by their failure at Bullecourt. There they were mere 'iron hulks', as one Digger described them. Another called them 'lumps of scrap metal'.

In general, the Australians knew little about mechanisation. Many

Diggers came from country districts where all transport was by horse and cart and where paddocks were still ploughed by horses pulling ploughshares. When they could actually get close to the Mark Vs they were interested in their construction, though one of the first questions on every Digger's lips was, 'Why do you call them tanks?' It was a natural mystification for men for whom tanks were cylindrical water containers. It was a matter of security, they were told. They looked as if they could hold water for battlefield supply so they were given the name tank to mislead German spies.

The tanks which came into service later in 1915 weighed forty tons and needed a crew of ten. The navy, which had much to do with the early development of the tank — though not with its concept — knew the tanks as 'landships'. The navy also supplied the first crews, but before long the army assumed control. On 15 December 1915 Captain H. W. Mortimore made history when he took tank D.1 into action at Delville Wood, Somme. Soon after, thirty-six tanks led British infantry in an attack against German defences at nearby Flers.

They terrified the Germans but Haig had allowed them to be used prematurely. They were still experimental and many broke down. Even more seriously, the secret of the tanks' existence was now out.

When they investigated the tanks, the Diggers, though impressed, were appalled by the heat, the noise and choking fumes inside the tanks. The crews gave them relatively easy rides but many of the men inside the beasts were bruised and shaken when they crashed into a ditch or over an obstacle. However, when British machine-guns were fired at the tanks to demonstrate their invulnerability to small arms fire some Diggers spoke of seeking a transfer into the Tank Corps!

But the monsters were still so new that in letters home and in diary entries about them the Diggers invariably referred to them as 'the Tanks', using inverted commas.

At Cambrai, 350 tanks had attacked on a front of twelve kilometres; at Hamel sixty covered a front of six-and-a-half kilometres, which at Cambrai would have been given about 175 tanks. The objective at Cambrai was very much deeper than that at Hamel, hence the greater density of tanks.

Monash, who treated war correspondents as intelligent allies rather than as nuisances, as the British generals regarded them, briefed Australian correspondents, including Bean, on 3 July. His most significant statement: 'If the tanks fail to get the strong points, the infantry cannot try. They are to let the tanks flatten out any serious opposition which they locate. They have been told, in such cases, to lie down and let the tank go ahead'.

Tanks did *not* get some strong points and it was unrealistic of Monash to suppose that his infantry would then hold back. An instruction not to try would have mystified them. When a tank was not available at the right time the Diggers overcame the obstacle in their own way.

Some tank officers stayed on foot and acted as links between infantry and tanks. When those officers spotted a likely target they took the initiative and directed a tank to the spot even before shouting to infantry to come up and join it. Major Burford Sampson gave the tanks passing but favourable mention in his diary entry on the day of battle. 'Tanks missed Pear [Trench] but did well.'

They did well elsewhere, too. A long communication trench ran east–west through Vaire Wood and finished up somewhere to the rear of the Germans' Hamel line. Known to the Australians as Huns Walk, it was the target of a joint action by platoons from the 13th and 15th Battalions supported by a tank.

All but three of the sixty tanks reached their objectives. By 11 am all but five had returned to their assembly points, eight kilometres to the rear. No tank was captured by the enemy, only one had been put out of action by German artillery and this, together with the others that had been 'missing', were returned within forty-eight hours. The Tank Corps had only thirteen casualties.

Apart from their late arrival, which was not caused by any fault of their own, the tanks performed as well as had been hoped, except on one dreadful occasion. The crew of a tank attached to the 43rd Battalion apparently lost direction, and while trying to regain it, came back towards its own infantry, firing at them. Of course, they scattered and officers wasted precious time in rallying them.

It had been thought in planning that in broad daylight and with the sun bright, the huge tanks would become easy targets for German planes and for the German 70 mm field artillery so, as arranged, they turned back to their base at 5.30 am, about two-and-a-half hours after the battle had commenced. But their influence remained behind, especially on the 6th Brigade's front at the southern end of the line. Here the tanks had terrified the Germans and caused such disarray that they retreated a full kilometre. The Diggers of the 25th Battalion took advantage of this to get their snipers into good positions. When the Germans tried to regain their lost ground after the tanks withdrew they came under sniper fire so accurate that they stayed at least 500 metres back from the Australian's new front.

For Brigadier Elles (soon promoted) and his officers, the Battle of Hamel had in effect been a sales demonstration for tanks, and it greatly influenced British generals and their planning staffs in preparing for the great offensive which was to begin on 8 August.

On 23 July, thirty-five British tanks supported a French division in a successful operation at Moreuil, not far from Hamel, in a direct copy of Monash's Hamel operation. In the same period, 18–26 July, the French Army used Schneiders, St Chamonds and Renaults to support French and American infantry at Soissons.

The Americans

According to Lieutenant E. J. Rule of the 14th Battalion, one of his men, on first meeting some Americans, said to one of them, 'Are you going to win the war for us, Yank?' There was incipient hostility in his voice because the Australians, in common with all the other Allied soldiers on the Western Front, believed that the United States should have been in the war much earlier than April 1917.

Even then their build-up in France was slow. General John Pershing, the American commander-in-chief, exasperated his European allies by refusing to commit his men until, he said, American action could be decisive. He irritated the French and British still further by his insistence that the American Expeditionary Force must operate independently. Having been horrified by the inadequacy of the Allies' leadership he did not want to entrust his men to leaders whose strategy and tactics had produced millions of casualties.

In May 1918 the AEF had taken part in battle for the first time, at least in a token role, and had captured Cantigny. According to widespread rumour, the Americans — variously called Yanks, Doughboys and Sammies — were boastful and brash. Hence, when Lieutenant Rule's Digger posed his question to the first American he met, he spoke with irony and sarcasm. But the American's answer was quick and tactful, 'Well, we just hope we'll fight as well as you'.

Right from the start, Diggers and Doughboys got along very well together and nowhere in official records or personal correspondence do Australians make any adverse criticisms of their American comrades at Hamel, other than noting their inexperience. They were willing, co-operative, courageous and enthusiastic.

American comments about themselves, so vainglorious during the Second World War, were reasonable and objective in 1918. The US 33rd Division HQ ordered each of its officers engaged at Hamel to produce a report immediately he returned to his unit after his experiences under Australian command. Whether short of lengthy — and most are long — they make interesting reading, as a selection of them shows.

Their comments about Australian soldiers are also important. For instance, the Australians had 'entire disregard for the personal property rights of prisoners of war'. The American officers might have said also that the Diggers had an entire disregard for their own safety when indulging their obsession for finding souvenirs. Several of the American leaders must have witnessed this extraordinary rashness. Perhaps they did not mention it out of tact.

Captain C. M. Gale, commanding Company C, 131st Infantry:
The system of messing the troops in advanced positions was very good, hot tea being provided twice each night and, in some of the trenches which were accessible, during the day. The handling of the mess was entirely through each company's first sergeant and by him to the platoons. [Gale meant the company sergeant major; an American 'first sergeant' was CSM equivalent.]

Captain W. J. Masoner, OC Company G, 132nd Infantry:
Our men acted like old veterans, were very eager to advance and had to be cautioned at different times to remain a sufficient distance in the rear of the barrage. The pace was very slow, about 100 yards per three minutes, many of the men stopping to light cigarettes ... One of my corporals and an

Australian went over to the German line, killed a German officer and brought back two prisoners carrying a machine-gun ... One of our stretcher-bearers was killed while carrying a white flag, being fired upon by a sniper.

Lieutenant E. K. Emerson, platoon commander Company F, 132nd Infantry:
The Australians commented favorably on the spirit and physical appearance of the men. They considered that our principal need was familiarity with firing of live grenades and actual target practice with Lewis guns. The relations between Americans and Australians was the best throughout our stay with them.

Captain Robert G. Hagan, 132nd Infantry, observing with AIF 21st Battalion:
From reports by officers of the AIF to whom our men were attached, our men gave an excellent account of themselves and did very effective work. They were well pleased with the way the men acted and with their spirit and morale.

Colonel J. B. Sanborn, CO 131st Infantry:
The 131st Infantry in the latter part of June were located in billets in towns near Eu, where they had been sent for training. Cadres of British officers were attached for this purpose. On the 21st the entire regiment was moved to Pierregot, northwest of Amiens, and there came under the training of the British 3rd Corps, with an Australian Division on their right. The Australians appeared to be more akin to our class in that they were an independent, alert, energetic lot of men and splendid fighters. From the first when our soldiers came in contact with them they mixed well and took kindly to each other ...

The battle of Hamel was the first engagement in which any troops of the 131st Infantry took part. The men went into the fight with great dash and maintained their courage to the end without any straggling. The Australians freely expressed themselves afterwards. The only complaint they could make was that our men were too savage and swift. They displayed remarkable dash and endeavored to be first and foremost in the fight. They did splendid work with the bayonet.

Captain C. M. Gale, OC Company C, 131st Infantry:
In the taking of German prisoners, a tendency was noted on part of Australian troops of an entire disregard for the personal property rights of

prisoners of war, stripping them as a rule of anything of value. It is feared that probably some of our troops followed this example ...

It is felt that more real good was done to this company by this operation with the Australians than could have been accomplished in months of training behind the lines.

Colonel Abel Davis, 132nd Infantry:
The following is the comment of the commander of the Australian battalion to which we were attached. 'The Americans attached to us deserve special mention for their part in the operation. They behaved wonderfully but were rather anxious to get rather close to our barrage, a common fault with new troops. There is not the slightest doubt that they possess all the qualifications to make first-rate fighting troops.'

Australian reports spoke highly of the Americans. The War Diary of the 6th Brigade noted: 'The Americans in the line are doing extremely well and are settling down to the new conditions quickly. All our officers and men speak highly of their cheerfulness, intelligence and rapid adaptability to strange surroundings. They are most eager to learn'.

But they never did learn Australian (and British) words of command; they were not required to. Diggers who watched the Yanks at drill could not stop themselves from laughing when they heard American orders, such as:

Australian version	American version
Slope arms!	Guys, muskets on your shoulders put!
Eyes right! (or left)	Guys, look at right! (or left)
Attention!	Guys, stop!
Stand at Ease!	Guys, slacken!

Despite these commands, strange to the Diggers' ears, they conceded that the Yanks' drill was almost as good as their own. For their part, the Americans noted that when the Diggers took their drill seriously they were impressive — but that they often did not take it seriously.

Philip Gibbs, the war correspondent, on the day after the battle, commented on the American troops:

One of the most interesting aspects of the action was the share taken in the fighting by American troops. There were not many of them compared with the Australians but the few companies were eager to go forward and meet the enemy face to face for the first time and to prove their fighting quality. They have proved up to the hilt of the sword their temper and their spirit and the Australian officers with whom I spoke yesterday and today told me that the Americans attacked with astonishing ardour, discipline and courage. If they had any fault, it was over-eagerness to advance so that they could hardly be restrained from going too rapidly behind the wide belt of our own shellfire as the barrage rolled forward.

It was the Fourth of July, the Day of American Independence, and many French villages quite close to the fighting lines were fluttering with the Tricolour and the Stars and Stripes in honour of their comradeship in arms. The Americans understood that upon their few companies fighting as platoons among the Australians rested the honour of the United States in this historic episode. They went forward with fixed bayonets, shouting the word 'Lusitania' as a battle-cry. Again and again the Australians heard that word on the American lips, as if there were something in the sound of it strengthening to the souls and terrifying to the enemy ... To American soldiers it is a cry for vengeance.

The *Lusitania* was a great passenger liner torpedoed by a German U-boat. This outrage was decisive in bringing the United States into the war.

Gibbs reported in detail on an action involving an American corporal aged twenty-one who was wounded three times but killed seven Germans. Gibbs wrote:

This tally, the boy reckons, is two Boches for each one wound and one over. He had an astounding series of episodes in which it was his life or the enemy's. After going through the enemy wire at Vaire Wood he found himself under fire from a machine-gun in a wheatfield and was wounded badly in the leg by an armour-piercing bullet designed for Tanks. He fell but staggering up again, threw a bomb at the German gun-crew and killed four of them. One ran and disappeared into a dugout. The American corporal followed him down and the man turned to leap at him in the darkness, but he killed him with his bayonet. He went up from the dugout to the light of day and a German soldier wounded him again but paid the price with his own life. Another German attacked him, wounded him for the third time, and was killed by this lad whose bayonet was so quick. That made six Germans and the seventh was a machine-gunner whom he shot. By this time the American corporal was weak and bleeding from his wounds and while he lay, unable to go further, he hoisted a rag on his rifle as a signal to the stretcher-bearers, who came and carried him away.

Gibbs also reported: 'Two Germans ran towards a young American corporal shouting 'Kamerad!' The corporal, not understanding that the word indicated surrender, would have killed them but an officer told him not to touch them. A little later he was wounded by a bullet and as he stumbled to his knees two Germans ran at him with bayonets. He had his finger on the trigger of his rifle and shot one of them dead, but the other drew near with his bayonet lowered.

[The corporal told Gibbs:] 'Then I knew I had to get up and fight like a man'. Despite his wound, he stood up and with his fixed bayonet turned aside the lunge which the German made to kill him and then swung up his rifle and cracked the man's skull.

It must be wondered to what extent this martial ruthlessness was the result of Australian advice and example.

The Australians set an example in another way — calmness under fire. Lieutenant Rule and an NCO found some Americans who had somehow lost their way on the Hamel battlefield.

We grabbed them [Rule wrote] and kept them in among our boys until they were relieved, I sat beside one of them during the bombardment and although he was game he was terrified. A look of wonder would spread over his face when a shell came pretty close and one of our lads would pass some remark, such as, 'Now then Fritz, cut that bloody game out, or you'll be killing someone'.

Such a comment may have seemed like nothing more than an attempt to cheer up an unblooded soldier, but it was more than that. The veteran Diggers had long since become ironically fatalistic. Few of them expected to survive the war without being wounded and the next enemy shell could be the one that did the damage. The Americans' part in the war ended four-and-a-half months later, on 11 November, Armistice Day. They had no time to become fatalistic as the Australians had done over a period of years, but they ended the war with a good reputation among their allies.

Field Marshal Haig awarded fourteen decorations to the officers and men of the US 131st and 132nd Infantry: four Military Crosses, including one to Lieutenant Frank Schram of the Medical Corps; four Distinguished Conduct Medals and six Military Medals. The most impressive citation was that for Corporal Thomas Pope's DCM:

At Hamel, on the evening of 4th July 1918, the enemy having captured one of our advanced posts by counter attacks, the first platoon of E Company was ordered to restore the position. Corporal Pope rushed a hostile machine-gun single-handed, bayoneted several of the crew and standing astride of a gun kept the remainder of the detachment at bay until the arrival of reinforcements and the gun-crew were all killed or captured.

Aeroplanes in Battle

The Royal Flying Corps had been renamed the Royal Air Force by the time of the Hamel battle and the Australian Flying Corps, though to a slight extent under its own command, was part of the RAF, though the AIF still referred to it as the AFC.

I have described the use of aircraft during the course of the battle, but other points need to be stressed. Among the novel activities of the pilots was the 'Strike a Light' patrol. By arrangement, they flew low over the Diggers as they reached new positions on the battlefield and tooted klaxon horns. This was the signal to the soldiers to strike matches or small flares, which they did in trenches or shell holes so that they would not be visible to the Germans.

From the air the AFC observer could clearly see rows of pinprick lights, which indicated the position of trenches, or in shell holes and behind cover, which indicated more scattered parties of soldiers. The observers marked these positions on a map, which they dropped at 4th Division HQ several minutes later. At least one ground observer on a high position, and able to see the tiny lights, confirmed the AFC observers' sightings. Hamel may have been the first occasion in military aviation history in which air observers 'honked' their own troops to 'strike a light'.

For the RAF the odds were heavily in favour of the enemy aircraft. The British-crewed ammunition carriers had to concentrate on that task while the Australian-crewed observation planes had to stick to their particular job. This was not a serious problem until the RAF fighters, whose principal duty had been to protect the bombers, withdrew with their charges about 9.30 am. The carriers and observers were then prey for the German squadrons which had been summoned to the scene. British and Australian airmen had machine-guns but they were unable at first to manoeuvre against the enemy pilots.

Having carried out their observation tasks, No. 3 Australian Squadron then turned on the Germans and fought them away from their main prey, the ammunition carriers. Nevertheless, the Germans machine-gunned Australian infantry in their new posts. Since the air combats and other activity took place at 1200 feet or less, the troops readily understood what the airmen were doing for them and they appreciated it. Few of the infantrymen would have changed places with the fliers. The Diggers, who were risking their lives every second, reckoned that war flying was too dangerous.

CHAPTER 12

Congratulations All Round and Suggestions for Monash

After the victory at Hamel became known telegrams were sent far and wide and none more importantly than to the Supreme War Council which was in session at Versailles, south-west of Paris. Present at the meeting were the prime ministers of France and Great Britain, Georges Clemenceau and David Lloyd George, Prime Minister Orlando of Italy, Prime Minister W. M. Hughes of Australia, numerous leading politicians, Field Marshal Haig, Chief of the Imperial General Staff Sir Henry Wilson, Marshal Ferdinand Foch, General John Pershing and many other leaders.

The prime ministers of Canada, New Zealand and Newfoundland asked Hughes to telegraph their congratulations to Monash. Clemenceau was dictating a telegram to a secretary and then decided to visit the Australians, specifically HQ 4th Division at Bussy-les-Daours, near Corbie. Here, on 7 July, Clemenceau and his staff were met by Rawlinson, Monash, Sinclair-MacLagan and other AIF senior officers.

According to C. E. W. Bean, he stood in the centre of a ring 'roughly formed by a number of Australians who had fought in the battle'. A number certainly, but as we know from candid officers such as Major Burford Sampson, of the 15th Battalion, and from others, the majority of the troops present were not Diggers who had been at Hamel but men drawn in to make up the numbers. Whoever they were, they gave Clemenceau a tremendous ovation after his complimentary remarks, which were to become famous. They are also enshrined on the Australian Corps Memorial at Hamel. (See page 5.)

Clemenceau spoke in morale-building language and his words were passed on to the AIF units in special orders. He was obviously sincere because he spoke in the grip of great emotion but, after two years' experience of the AIF in France and Belgium, he knew that the Diggers reacted favourably to praise.

Praise and congratulations reached Monash from many other sources, including King George V, who visited France to bestow honours and awards, among them the decorations given to American soldiers.

Haig sent a telegram to Rawlinson:

Will you please convey to Lieutenant General Sir John Monash and all ranks under his command, including the tanks and the detachment of American troops, my warm congratulations on the success which attended the operations carried out this morning and on the skill and gallantry with which they were conducted.

For Brigadier Elles, promoted to major general, Hamel was 'certainly the most successfully executed small battle of all arms'. As GOC Tank Corps he was in a position to know. He modestly took some credit for the success, not only because of the efficiency of his Corps, but also because he felt that GHQ had heeded his insistence that it should be enterprisingly aggressive and not always taking defensive measures.

The Tank Corps officers were impressed by the Australians. Brigadier Courage spoke for his corps: 'All tank officers were much impressed with the superb morale of the Australian troops, who never considered that the presence of tanks exonerated them from fighting and took instant advantage of any opportunity created by the tanks'.

The depth of the Australians' new respect for the tanks and their crews was clear in reports sent in by battalion commanders.

Lieutenant Colonel E. A. Drake-Brockman, 16th Battalion, wrote: 'The tanks were particularly useful and efficient'. This was a remarkable admission from an officer whose unit had suffered so grievously at Bullecourt as a result of the tanks' inefficiency. According to Lieutenant Colonel T. P. McSharry: 'One tank saved us a great number of casualties at the final objective. This tank gave an ideal illustration of co-operation with infantry'.

Lieutenant Colonel D. G. Marks, 13th Battalion also considered the tank's potential: 'I feel sure that tanks, when so ably used, could obviate the necessity for a final protective barrage and leave more scope for exploiting success. They even appeared to anticipate to infantry's desires'.

Monash's own divisional and brigade commanders congratulated him, though Sinclair-MacLagan justifiably felt that some of the credit should go to him as he had been the operational commander.

Further north along the British front line, commanders soon heard of the triumph. They then knew little about the details of the action but the word 'success' had been so rarely heard that it was a welcome relief. It certainly heartened the French on the Australians' right. Even more to Monash's liking, news of his coup was published and welcomed in Australia.

Rawlinson also congratulated Monash, while making it clear that he himself was the real victor of Hamel. It is worth making the point here that Rawlinson was anti-Semitic, as was his chief of staff, Major General A. A. Montgomery. Monash saw both men almost daily but they concealed their anti-Semitism from him. P. A. Pedersen, in his magnificently researched *Monash as a Military Commander*, makes Rawlinson's attitude clear from two 'acrid' letters Rawlinson wrote to Montgomery in 1920 when he believed that Sir Edwin Montague, also a Jew, might oppose his appointment as Commander-in-Chief India. Pedersen quotes some of Rawlinson's comments:

I read him as a clever, slippery, creepy crawly Jew who will always back you if he thinks you are winning and have no scruples about sticking you in the back if he thinks you look like a loser. He is clever and intelligent but his knees knock together when trouble is about. Edwin is not unlike Monash! We know how to manage his sort.

Monash was congratulated in person by Billy Hughes. Hughes had called on Monash at his HQ on 2 July and with Sir Joseph Cook, Minister for the Navy, addressed some of the troops, about 200 each from the 4th, 11th and 6th Brigades, as well as No. 3 Squadron AFG. While Monash, who was naturally very busy with the imminent Hamel operation, regarded the PM's visit as a nuisance, what Hughes and Cook had to say was morale-boosting for the men.

While resenting the PM's intrusion at such a time, Monash nevertheless asked him to consult the AIF generals separately about the command structure of the AIF. Apparently, nearly every officer to whom he spoke said that the arrangement that Monash should control the corps and Birdwood the administration would work efficiently.

For the morale of the troops, the visit of Hughes and Cook could not have come at a better time. The soldiers took to Hughes, whom they called 'the little Digger' — from his diminutive size. When he visited the groups of soldiers he took every opportunity, while his colleague Cook was speaking, to lie on the grass while chewing a blade of grass and looking into the faces of the men. An observer said that the PM seemed 'wrapped up in the men'.

Bean gives what he calls 'the kernel' of Hughes' message to the men:

Your deeds, the history of this war, are the basis upon which the nation of Australians will be brought up. You have fought to keep alive the ideal of freedom and to save Australia from the domination to which, if Germany won, we would certainly be subjected. While you are doing that abroad we pledge ourselves to look after your interests at home.

Cook's pledge was that, after the war, Australia had a fine repatriation and veterans' welfare scheme waiting for the troops when they returned. He claimed that it would be the finest plan that any country had drawn up, and so it proved to be.

Monash and Major General George Bell, GOC 33rd American Division, exchanged compliments, with Bell echoing Monash.

Monash to Bell:

I desire to take the opportunity of tendering to you, as their immediate commander, my earnest thanks for the assistance and services of the four companies of infantry who participated in yesterday's brilliant operations. The dash, gallantry and efficiency of these American troops left nothing to be desired, and my Australian soldiers speak in the very highest terms in praise of them. That soldiers of the United States and of Australia should have been associated for the first time in such close co-operation on the battlefield is an historic event of such significance that it will live forever in the annals of our respective nations.

Bell to Monash:

The bravery, efficiency and skill of Australian soldiers are fully appreciated by this Division and they are known to the whole world. That your soldiers should have spoken in high terms of our men is the highest praise they could wish for. To have fought on the battlefield with Australia, in the brilliant operation of July the fourth, will remain forever an historic event in the annals of our country.

Rawlinson, in writing to Bell, allowed himself an implicit criticism of Haig:

Am anxious to express to you, General Bell, and to all ranks of the 33rd (Illinois) Division my warm thanks for the gallant part taken by portions of your division in the attack at Hamel and Vaire Wood on Independence Day. I hear nothing but praise for the manner in which your units fought the enemy and *my only regret is that I was not permitted to employ a larger portion of your fine division*. Perhaps later there may be another opportunity. [emphasis added]

There was never to be another opportunity for Rawlinson to exercise command over American troops. General Pershing was the one senior commander who had reservations about the Hamel operation. While tokenistically applauding Monash's victory he remained displeased that his orders that Americans were not to take part had been disobeyed. He learned only on 5 July that four American companies of the 33rd Division had been involved, and this was 'somewhat of a surprise' he said in his memoirs.

Pershing told Haig that all future plans to use his men before they were fully trained were to be referred to him personally and he repeated his desire to have direct control over American formations operating on the Western Front. Hearing of this, Rawlinson, who needed fresh blood after the loss of so much British blood and recognised the great potential of the Americans as soldiers, called on Haig for a ruling. What he got was a piece of Haig double-talk: 'United States units attached to the British for training will act as integral parts of the British units and they may take part in any fighting in which those units are involved'. But then came the caveat: 'They must not be specially attached for the purpose of taking part'.

In the event, only two American divisions came directly under British command, the 27th and the 30th, during operations in the Ypres Salient in 1918.

Soon after the plaudits came criticisms, suggestions and recommendations, all of them thoughtful and constructive. Many were acted upon by Monash, his staff and his senior subordinates. Some of the suggestions came from American officers who had been engaged in the operation.

Extracts from the lengthy report sent in by AIF 11th Brigade show the serious and helpful nature of the criticisms. They also reflect the serious approach to his job of Brigadier J. H. Cannan, the brigade commander. Bean regarded the 11th as 'the happiest brigade in the AIF'. In a corps where all commanders were considerate about their men, Cannan was outstanding.

Forward Observation Officers

The FOO's did not appear to do much; they appeared to lack communication with their batteries. Cannot each Artillery Brigade or Group concentrate on providing at least one FOO with more or less reliable communications by means of visual or line? Many useful targets were missed by reason of this lack of communication.

The Attack

The chief thing noticed during the actual assault was that men were attracted to the scene of a local fight with the result that gaps in our line occurred. It is considered that such gaps should be filled by the Reserve Tanks following the infantry until such time as the Infantry Commander redistributes his men. This is merely a matter of arrangement and co-operation with the tanks detailed for the operation.

Action of the Tanks

The support and covering fire given by the tanks was of great value but their capabilities were limited and they were exposed to a greater chance of being hit owing to the advancing barrage and the slow rate at which it moved.

Keeping Direction

In newly captured country bare of distinctive landmarks it is difficult to accurately locate oneself on the map and it is suggested that on prominent features behind our original line large beacons be lit to assist the troops. In order to avoid any confusion as to which beacon one is looking at perhaps it could be arranged for them to be of different colours.

Depth of Attack

It is considered that strongly held tactical features should not be allowed to hang up an advance but that special parties be detailed to engage them, if necessary attacking them in reverse after the leading wave has passed and joined up beyond them.

If it is desirable to have a halt in the barrage it is considered that either the rate of fire should be decreased or the guns should cease to fire altogether. In the latter case the halt should be fairly lengthy so that the foremost troops may have an opportunity of dealing with any enemy who are in their immediate vicinity.

Transport

Difficulty was experienced in guiding regimental transport to localities in the newly captured position. It is therefore suggested that the Transport Sergeant and a few drivers live at Battalion HQ during an operation and during the hours of daylight go out and reconnoitre the new area so that they may be able to bring up the transport without requiring any guides.

Exploiting Success

Nothing of this nature was allowed by higher authority although suggestions for the mopping up of certain batteries were put up prior to Zero. When the final objective had been captured there were no enemy within 1000 yards of it during the hours of daylight following and the quietness of the enemy's artillery was apparently due to his withdrawing his batteries. Had any exploiting of success been allowed it is almost certain that at little cost to ourselves many more casualties would have been inflicted on the enemy and many more enemy guns captured.

[Author's note: This is Brigadier Cannan himself speaking, not an officer on his staff. He had disagreed with Monash about the degree of exploitation following capture of the objective. In this observation he is, in effect, saying to his chief, 'There, I told you so'.]

Frontage

The frontage allotted this brigade was approximately 2000 yds, which was about 1 man per yard taking into account the four battalions of the brigade plus the 2 companies U.S. Infantry attached, but one battalion was in reserve and not employed — hence in the actual attack there was less than one man per yard. This strength per yard was considerably below that generally considered necessary but proved to be quite sufficient.

Artillery

As far as infantry are concerned, they prefer a H.E. [high explosive] barrage to a shrapnel one. It is stated that shrapnel shells bursting overhead cause much apprehension among the troops. While the 'whirr' of the shrapnel frightens the enemy and keeps his head down it is considered that this effect is obtained by use of overhead M.G. fire. An H.E. barrage is only effective when the ground is hard.

It is considered that in future operations which involve the capture of well defined and well sited trench systems the final objective should be well away from such systems, which should be avoided by as many troops as possible. The dugouts in the system captured gave protection to a portion of the garrison but were not sufficient for everybody.

It is considered that the pace of the barrage was too slow, particularly at first. If a close assembly in or forward of our front line is being carried out it is essential that the barrage advance rapidly so as to enable all assaulting troops to clear our front line and shake out into attack formation before the enemy's barrage comes down.

In order to allow of local exploiting of a success and at the same time mislead the enemy as to the most forward line being consolidated, the following is a suggestion. As part of the pre-arranged artillery program after the protective barrage for the final objective had been down for say 20 minutes, it will again commence to advance for about 700 yards by 100-yard lifts. The infantry if they desire can either not move at all or closely follow the barrage or go out after the barrage ... Such a local exploiting of success would allow of our new frontline to be sited as best suited for local tactics. [The point is developed at length.]

[Author's note: Again, this is Cannan's personal opinion and what he suggested was eminently sensible. However, it was not Monash's way to permit exploitation which he himself had not approved in his master plan. In this there was at least one weakness in this brilliant soldier's approach to battle.]

Orders and Instructions

With the experience now gained by all commanders it is considered that many of the Orders and instructions for operations should be cut out, all points for discussion being settled at a conference for those concerned. In this operation instructions were received too late for issue to units. If instructions by Brigade come from higher authority the former must for its own protection pass them on in writing to units, [but] this limits the initiative of unit commanders and throws a great amount of office work onto the staff and clerks when the former would be better employed reconnoitring the area of operations.

[Author's note: Here Cannan makes another dig at Monash and at Sinclair-MacLagan, his direct 'higher authority' for the Hamel operation. For Cannan, as for others, there were too many orders from superiors who, once action had been joined, were not necessarily in the best position to know what was happening in the forward area.]

If Monash felt any resentment at the suggestions and criticisms that reached him, he had only himself to blame. He had demanded intelligent thought and enterprise from his subordinates — and he was getting it. After all, they had given him his victory.

CHAPTER 13

The Rare Process of Analysing Success

The War Office and certain training commands, through the office of the Chief of the Imperial General Staff, as well as GHQ in France, often produced pamphlets, studies and 'Intelligence Summaries' concerning operations and developments, but no Authority had had much experience of analysing success. Staff officers whose task it was to produce studies had brought out valuable training papers but, in relation to operations, they had been forced to use their talents in making defeats seem like successes and to explain that retreats had actually been 'strategic withdrawals'. With the Hamel operation they had a genuine victory to analyse and this must have been a rare satisfaction.

The army pamphlet, *Operations by the Australian Corps Against Hamel, Bois de Hamel and Bois de Vaire*, published in the same month as the battle, summarised the orders and events. Of greatest interest are its conclusions about the success of the operation:

a   The care and skill as regards every detail with which the plan was drawn up by the Corps, Division, Brigade and Battalion staffs.

b   The excellent co-operation between the infantry, machine-gunners, artillery, tanks and the RAF.

c   The complete surprise of the enemy resulting from the manner in which the operation had been kept secret up till zero hour.

d   The precautions which were taken and successfully carried out, by which no warning was given to the enemy by any previous activity which was not normal.

e   The effective counter-battery work and accurate barrage.

f   The skill and dash with which the tanks were handled and the care taken over details in bringing them up to the starting line.

g   Last, but most important of all, the skill, determination and fine fighting spirit of the infantry carrying out the attack.

Another GHQ 'Staff Paper' stated: 'The value of tanks in assisting infantry to advance is conclusively proved'. This study gave six main reasons for the success:

- secrecy during planning;
- thoroughness of planning;
- determination and tactical handling of platoons;
- high morale of the Australians;
- relatively poor enemy defences; and
- hard ground on which the tanks could operate effectively.

GHQ published an Intelligence Summary on 5 August which included a short account of the Hamel operation under the heading 'Notes on Recent Fighting'. The key passage is perhaps this one:

Success was largely due to the determination of the infantry and to the tactical handling of platoons. The infantry fought its way forward, making use of its own weapons when the co-operation of the other arms was not available. In drawing deductions from this action it is important to bear in mind the local and special conditions, the high morale of the infantry, the fact that there was not much wire, that the ground was suitable for the action of tanks and that the objective was strictly limited and within the effective fire of the field and heavy artillery as sited for the attack.

Nobody seems to have made the point, either then or later, that the Diggers did not just use their own weapons — they used those of the enemy. At battalion, company and platoon level officers had ensured that their men were taught how to operate the Maxim machine-gun in particular. Many a captured machine-gun was turned on the enemy and there were times when the Maxim was used after the Vickers had run out of ammunition. Similarly, the Diggers were taught how to handle the German Mauser rifle and pistol as well as the enemy mortars, and they were instructed in the characteristics of German grenades. The Australians had a natural curiosity in the equipment used by everybody on the Western Front and they readily understood new mechanisms. They preferred their own SMLE rifles and Lewis guns but they said that the German Maxim machine-gun was better than the British Vickers.

Monash, never a man to be modest when he had done something to be proud of, penned a description of Hamel which became famous. I have already referred to this passage but it bears repeating: 'A perfected modern battle plan is like nothing so much as a score for an orchestral composition, where the various arms and units are the instruments, and the tasks they perform are their respective musical phrases'.

C. E. W. Bean expressed himself more journalistically. Hamel was 'a big battle on a small scale'. Everything necessary for a major battle had been used. However we measure 'big', Hamel was certainly Monash's first big test as corps commander and he knew he had come through it with distinction.

Bean gave Hamel much thought and in 1942, in his *Official History, Volume VI*, he stated that the chief importance of the battle lay 'in its being an exercise for the British command and troops for the offensive which all expected to occur when, that year or next, the balance of strength finally turned against the enemy'. For Bean, Hamel could not have been the success it was without the daring and efficiency of infantry and tank crews. 'Two hours at Hamel,' he wrote, 'completed a revolution in the Diggers' opinion, which never afterwards changed'.

To what extent Hamel made the British commanders more offensive-minded can hardly be measured. Clemenceau's public, vehement and enthusiastic praise for the Australian victory may have encouraged Haig and his Army commanders, although generally anything that the French leaders advocated Haig automatically rejected. P. A. Pedersen considers that the change in Allied thinking began on 18 July when Mangin's Tenth Army and Degoutte's Sixth Army destroyed Ludendorff's last great offensive.

This battle near Soissons was immense. In round figures, the French employed 24 division, 2000 guns, 1100 aircraft and 500 tanks; they captured 15 000 prisoners, 400 guns and advanced nine-and-a-half kilometres. This victory gets scant mention in British histories of the war. Pedersen's assessment could be right, but Haig had called Hamel 'quite a nice success' and it is tempting to think that it began a new process of offensive thought in his mind. If nothing else, he had to admit that the Australians had gained a moral superiority over the Germans and that they had demonstrated that German defences could be broken, a heartening realisation for all the Allied leaders, political and military.

On 1 July, three days before the battle, Haig had visited Monash at his HQ to discuss the coming operation and later noted, 'Monash is a most capable commander who thinks out every detail on an operation and leaves nothing to chance'. This was true, but chance plays a large part in any fighting and, on such occasions, Monash's success was dependent on his junior leaders in the field, and especially on those who dared to deviate from the detailed plan in an emergency. One of the 'details' laid down was that when the advance was held up the infantry should lie down and wait for the tanks. But had they 'laid down' in front of Pear Trench and waited for the tanks the battle would certainly have taken longer and could have been much more costly.

Captain R. Glasgow of the 15th Battalion and Lieutenant J. J Dwyer of 4th MG Company saved many lives through the skilful way in which they handled the troops around them. Major Burford Sampson of the 15th observed in his diary entry for 7 July, 'Captain Glasgow showed out above others when the line was held up at Pear Trench'. Glasgow, aged thirty-one, had been a station hand at Gympie, Queensland, on enlistment; Dwyer, aged twenty-eight, was only a labourer from Alonnah, South Bruny Island, Tasmania. In the AIF, status and profession in civil life had no relevance to rank achieved. Glasgow finished the war with the awards of DSO and MC, Dwyer won the supreme award, the VC.

Australian soldiers recognised an able leader the moment they set eyes on him. Captain Fred Woods, the gallant company commander of 16th Battalion, had been a miner at Broken Hill but this background as a manual labourer had neither hindered his advancement nor affected the respect his men had for him. Had he not been killed at Hamel, he would almost certainly have risen to command a battalion.

In the matter of junior leadership, the US Army of the time was closely similar to the AIF. Probably the best qualified witness to this was Brigadier (later Major General) C. M. Wagstaff, who spent the first half of the war with the AIF at Gallipoli and then with the 5th Division on the Western Front, and the second half as the British representative attached to American GHQ. He wrote:

The two forces were the nearest thing possible to each other. Their discipline is founded on the personal influence of the officer over his men. They have to rely upon the character and personality of the officer, and, provided that they get the right class of officer, there is no trouble whatever with their discipline any more than with ours.

Wagstaff's use of the word 'class' may be misleading but he made it clear, in amplification of his comments, that he was not referring to social class but to 'class of leadership'.

All the contemporary comments emphasised the platoon leading. This was tribute to the quality of the lieutenants and sergeants who commanded those platoons. This being the Australian Army, virtually all these junior leaders had come up from the ranks and were therefore veterans at their job. In addition, numerous private soldiers readily assumed command when their officers and NCOs were knocked out of action. The AIF private soldier who took over an American platoon was another example of initiative of the kind which the reports spoke about.

Various soldiers and specialist historians have assessed Monash and speculated on what he might have become after Hamel. This in itself is interesting because he was only a lieutenant general at the war's end, one of hundreds of officers of this rank. Above him were scores of full generals and some field marshals.

A. J. P. Taylor, in 1963, said of Monash: 'He was the only general of creative originality produced by the First World War'. And Taylor meant of any nationality.

Captain Basil Liddell Hart, one of the most eminent of British historians of The First World War, considered Monash 'the most outstanding Corps commander of the War'.

Field Marshal Montgomery, in 1968, wrote:

I could name Sir John Monash as the best general on the Western Front in Europe. He possessed real creative originality, and the war might well have been over sooner and with fewer casualties, had Haig been relieved of his command and Monash appointed to command the British Army in his place.

David Lloyd George also wrote about Monash in his memoirs after the war:

The only soldier thrown up on the British side who possessed the necessary qualities was a Dominion General [Monash]. Competent professional soldiers whom I have consulted have all agreed that this man might and probably would have risen to the height of the occasion. But I knew nothing of this at the time.

Major General E. K. G. Sixsmith told Pedersen:

Of one thing I am certain, if Monash had been C-in-C the scientific study of the attack in trench warfare would have been undertaken much more actively and sooner than under Haig. But that is an unreal supposition because it was late in 1916 — after the casualties on the Somme — that these studies should have been started — and Monash had certainly not achieved command status by that time.

Sixsmith also makes the highly pertinent observation that Monash would not have had the authority to 'command men of experience and ability such as Rawlinson, Plumer and Byng'.

Whatever Monash's command potential, it was never remotely possible that he would become C-in-C. Innumerable generals were superior to him in rank and it would have been inconceivable in the climate of the time for a dominion general to have been given supreme command. The final obstacle would have been King George V, who was Haig's protector. It is wrong to suggest that Monash, however brilliant, was any more 'original' and creative than, say, the British General Sir Ivor Maxse, GOC BEF 18th Corps. Maxse was regarded as the finest trainer of British soldiers of his period. Another great British Corps Commander was Lieutenant General Sir Claud Jacob.

Monash should certainly have been promoted to the rank of full General. He constantly controlled more troops and carried out far more important operations than his predecessor, Birdwood, who was a general and later promoted field marshal.

Monash's command from August 1918 was immense. First there were his own five infantry divisions, three other divisions, then 50 000 Corps troops. Among the units concerned were the 13th Australian Light Horse Regiment, two Australian tunnelling companies, siege, heavy artillery and heavy mortar, transport and signal units, motor-ambulance convoys, about twenty 'Labour Companies', and even the 3rd Squadron AFC. These able airmen were permanently attached to Monash's command and he used them as he had at Hamel — for reconnaissance, contact patrols and artillery spotting. Monash had under his command at least 160 000 men, and his corps may have been the largest of the BEF's twenty corps. He wrote:

My command is more than two and half times the size of the British Army under the Duke of Wellington, or of the French Army under Napoleon Bonaparte, at the Battle of Waterloo. Moreover, I have in the Army Corps an artillery which is more than six times as numerous and more than one hundred times as powerful as that commanded by the Duke of Wellington.

This colourful comparison is not particularly meaningful, as warfare had developed beyond any possible comparison between 1815 and 1918. However, Monash's statement admirably serves to demonstrate his pride in his command.

The statistics which pertain to the period of Monash's command of the Australian Corps I quote without analysis. The Diggers suffered 21 243 casualties, one-fifth of them being killed. They took 29 144 prisoners, 338 artillery pieces, hundreds of trench mortars and possibly thousands of machine-guns — the exact figure is impossible to assess. They liberated from the Germans 116 towns and villages in an area of 865 square kilometres. According to Pedersen's calculations, these figures represent about 22 per cent of the captures of the entire British Army in the final phase of the war on the Western Front.

In historical truth, it must be admitted that Monash exaggerated his claims for the Hamel of Battle. This was the result of natural pride and a tactical desire to heighten even further his own credibility and that of his soldiers as fine fighting men. Monash asserted that he had undertaken the Hamel operation to boost public spirits and morale; he probably had the Australian public in mind. He also said that he intended to prompt higher commanders to think offensively. Hamel certainly had this effect but Monash could hardly claim that this had been his incentive. Hamel was undertaken for limited tactical reasons. It was nonetheless spectacular and important for that.

Monash's claim that his incentive had been to make his superiors more offensive has been disputed by some British historians. Also, debate has taken place about his 'inventing' the tactics employed at Hamel. The historian Denis Winter states, in his book *Haig's Command*, that the tactics were copied from a GHQ document, SS135. If so, it is remarkable that GHQ in general and Haig in person did not claim credit for the victory at Hamel.

CHAPTER 14

Australian Corps Memorial Park
Unique Among War Memorials

The concept of an Australian Battlefield Memorial Park was mine, in 1960, as was its site. However, the design, interpretation and features of the Park were the product of many skilful and imaginative minds and the result of much hard work by various people. The designer was Mr D. M. Taylor, of Sydney.

Only a small part of the park is Australian-owned, but that part is significant since it is the heart of the park and incorporates some of the original 1918 trenches captured from the Germans by the Diggers who turned them into their own forward trenches.

The Memorial Park does not exist in isolation but as part of an Australian 1918 Battlefield Tour, which traces the period from March to July 1918. While it could be commenced at any intermediate point, it is best begun at Victoria School, Villers-Bretonneux, and concluded at the Australian Corps Memorial Park.

The Anzac Museum within the Victoria School has an audio-visual theatre and visitors should watch the documentary *The Fighting Spirit: Hamel, The Turning Point* to gain a full understanding of the events of 1918 and of the Diggers themselves. The executive producer of the film was Colonel (later Brigadier) Kevin O'Brien, the director was Geoff Barnes, the editor Kate Ryan, and the historical commentator and on-screen presenter, John Laffin.

The film was made by the Australian Army Training Command, not as an army instructional film but for a general Australian audience. Other purely military aspects of the Battle of Hamel I covered in extra footage decided on by Kevin O'Brien, for example, the subject of defending a reverse slope, which the Germans did at Pear Trench.

The tour route is well signposted and a battlefield tour guide and cassette is available. You do not need to stop at each of the sixteen locations but you do need to listen to the cassette at the stops indicated in the guide. A quick tour takes half a day so it is better to stay overnight in the area, so you can watch the video one evening and drive the tour next day. Remember, this is the most significant Australian memorial and it is worth your time.

1. Villers-Bretonneux School
The original school was destroyed by shellfire in March/April 1918 but was rebuilt with donations provided by the children of the State of Victoria and reopened in 1927. The museum houses an interesting exhibition of Australian artefacts and a photographic collection. Visiting hours: Monday to Saturday 4 pm–6 pm; Sunday, 10 am–12 noon. Call at the Town Hall (Mairie) for a visit outside these hours.

2. Villers-Bretonneux Château
After leaving the school return to N29 and turn left towards Amiens. After 150 metres the ruins of the former château are on the right. It was occupied by several armies. After the second battle for Villers-Bretonneux, 24–27 April 1918, the château was used by senior AIF officers who helped to plan the great offensive of 8 August 1918. Later it was occupied by the Australian Graves Unit.

3 Adelaide Cemetery
Continue one kilometre along the N29 Amiens road; the cemetery is on the right, on the outskirts of Villers-Bretonneux. Begun in June 1918, the cemetery contains the graves of 519 Diggers killed between March and September 1918. The remains of the Unknown Australian Soldier were exhumed from Adelaide Cemetery in 1993 and were reinterred in the Australian War Memorial.

4. Australian National War Memorial
The Australian National War Memorial is on the D23–Villers-Bretonneux–Fouilloy road and this necessitates a return from Adelaide Cemetery into Villers-Bretonneux. Do not attempt a U-turn on the N29, which is a busy and dangerous road. First, continue towards Amiens and turn around at the crossroads of the N29–D523. In Villers-Bretonneux, turn left towards the signposted memorial. The Villers-Bretonneux Military Cemetery contains 779 Australians, as well as British, Canadian,

South African and New Zealand servicemen. The National Memorial is across a convex slope and is not visible until you walk part of the way through the cemetery. On the screen wall of the memorial are the names of 10 982 men who were killed in France and who have no known marked grave. The tower of the memorial is often open for access and the spectacular view of the Somme uplands makes the climb worthwhile.

5. Village of Hamelet

From the National Memorial continue north to Fouilloy and on its outskirts turn right into the D623, signposted Hamelet. After 300 metres take the D91 at a crossroads. In the fields to your left and right as you reach Hamelet, thirty of the tanks of the 5th Tank Brigade assembled on 3 July to support the Diggers in their attack at Hamel. Suggestion: In the centre of Hamelet, park in the square and here play the first part of the audio guide cassette. In and around Hamelet, sixty British Mark V battle tanks and four supply tanks assembled on 3 July, moving off at a crawl at 10.30 pm on 3 July. Walk 100 metres down the D71 to the edge of the Hamelet settlement. Le Hamel is about three kilometres distant, at 2 o'clock from the axis of the road.

6. Pear Trench

Continue on the D71 to Vaire-sous-Corbie, turn right at the crossroads and follow D71 towards Le Hamel. After 200 metres, at a fork in the road, is a crucifix. Take the right fork here for one-and-a-half kilometres until you reach another crucifix at another fork. Park and listen to the second section of the cassette. Walk up the slope along the narrow unsealed sunken road for 800 metres. You are now at Pear Trench, in the German front line at the moment of the AIF attack. Look south-west and you will imagine the AIF front line crossing the sunken road just below the crest. Fifty metres over this crest, unseen by the Diggers, was the strongly defended Pear Trench.

The artillery barrage commenced 100 metres ahead of the attack start line. The 43rd Battalion (3rd Division) advanced up the rise to your left; the 15th Battalion (1st Division) advanced on your right. As they advanced, the 15th especially found the enemy wire uncut by the barrage and the men of the unit crawled and scrambled through the barbed wire, all the while under fire from enemy machine-guns. Here, just to the right of the road, Private Harry Dalziel, 15th Battalion, won the VC. Return to your car and take the sealed road to the top of the hill.

7. AIF Front and Start Line

You will come to Site No. 7. Here the AIF 4th Brigade front line crossed the road; it was also the boundary between the 15th and 16th Battalions. In the field 100 metres to the left was the start line of the 16th Battalion. A further 200 metres across from the line of the sunken road was the German front line. It ran south to the crossroads at Vaire Wood, then followed the road around the front of this wood past the quarry and continued on towards the Fouilloy–Lamotte–Warfusée road. The 16th Battalion's task on 4 July was to capture and clear Vaire and Hamel Woods. On today's maps the two woods are shown as a single feature, Vaire Wood.

8. Australian Start Line

Between Sites 7 and 8 you have been following a road which ran parallel with the AIF front line. Follow this road to its junction with the D122. The start line for the 13th Battalion (4th Division) crossed the intersection of the D122 and the Fouilloy–Lamotte–Warfusée road. The battalion had to seize the furthest edge of the spur, 250 metres beyond Vaire Wood. The actions of the 13th and 15th Battalions are described in my account of the battle.

9. The German Front Line

Turn left into the D122 and after 100 metres turn left again into the Villers-Bretonneux–Le Hamel road. The German front line ran along the right side of this road for 200 metres, then crossed over and continued down the hill around the front of Vaire Wood and passing Kidney Trench before making a left turn to head up the line of the sunken road to Pear Trench. The 16th Battalion advanced through this area on 4 July, clearing and securing Vaire and Hamel Woods. Park at the junction where the sunken road to Pear Trench meets the Le Hamel road (Site No 10). Now listen to the third section of the cassette. You now face a short walk to view the site of Kidney Trench and Vaire Wood.

10. Kidney Trench & Vaire Wood Walks

Two short and interesting walks may be made. The first is back along the sunken road immediately in front of Vaire Wood to view the site of the

German redoubt known as Kidney Trench. The second is into the wood to view the location of the enemy communication trench known to the Diggers as Huns Walk. For the location of Kidney Trench, walk back to the bend in the sunken road in front of Vaire Wood. In the field opposite and between the northern end of the small wooded area called Central Copse, notice a lighter patch of soil. This was the site of Kidney Trench where Lance Corporal Thomas Axford, 16th Battalion, won the VC.

Near this bend in the road were many dugouts from which numerous German prisoners as well as trench mortars were captured by the 16th Battalion.

11. Huns Walk

Walking through the wood, you will see the line of the long communication trench, Huns Walk, which ran from Kidney Trench east to Accroche Wood. When you leave the southern end of the wood, just past the fork in the road, is an open area to your right, bordered on two sides by the wood. The centre of this area was the site of one of the four resupply dumps used by the carrier tanks. Further up the rise is an ammunition drop zone used by the Royal Flying Corps and the Australian Flying Corps.

12 & 13 Australian Objectives

Back in your vehicle, continue towards Le Hamel. After 150 metres turn sharp right at the V-shaped junction into the small sealed road that takes you through Vaire Wood, passing the re-supply dump and air-drop zone, until you reach Site No 12. Near this signpost pull up and listen to the fourth part of the tape. This road intersection was near the line of the final objective, which ran north-east past Accroche Wood then north-east past Le Hamel and the Australian Corps Memorial Park. It then continued north-east across the Somme River. You are now in the area of the new front line held by the AIF until the Allied offensive of 8 August 1918.

Continue east to the junction with the D122. Turn left onto this road for about half a kilometre; now turn left again at the next sealed road to Le Hamel village. Two kilometres towards the village you again cross the line of the AIF's objective. At the same time you intersect Huns Walk where it ran from Vaire Wood to Accroche Wood. Another kilometre beyond, in the fields to your left, was a second tank resupply point and air-drop zone. On the right were German support trenches which ran north along the ridge through Accroche Wood towards Le Hamel. They formed part of the German defence line called Wolfsberg.

Continue north along the D122. The road dips and Le Hamel lies to the left.

14. Hamel Approach
Site No. 14 is beside a small chapel. Park and here listen to the fifth part of the cassette. The 43rd Battalion and its tanks attacked through Le Hamel, clearing out the Germans. The 44th, operating on the 43rd's left but clear of the village, headed for a knot of trenches on and beyond the ridge crest east of the village. The German position they took was the Wolfsberg Command Post and it is appropriately now the site of the Australian Corps Memorial Park.

15. Le Hamel
On entering Le Hamel, turn left at the French memorial in the middle of the road and proceed to the church. Outside is the Ross Bastiaan plaque, with its description of the battle exploit. Much of the village around you was in ruins in 1918 but some buildings are recognisable from a comparison of old and modern photographs, as shown in the guide brochure.

16. The Australian Corps Memorial Park
Return to the French memorial in its triangular traffic island, turn left, drive fifty metres and turn right at an Australian signpost to drive up the new narrow sealed road to the Memorial Park. It is a significant site, being the final objective of the Diggers' attack on 4 July. It is a majestic memorial, with many descriptive plaques, with texts in English and French, to inform visitors about the course of the battle and matters of associated interest, such as the site of the shooting down of Baron von Richthofen, the 'Red Baron'.

I suggest that you take special note of the colour patches of every unit of the AIF, glazed onto the top of the low walls around the memorial itself, with its great Rising Sun Badge sandblasted onto Australian granite by Melbourne stonemason Colin Anderson. It challenges the attention.

The capture of Le Hamel and the German lines was not the end of the story. On 8 August, five weeks after the exploit, the Australian Corps advanced from this site in the attack that the mastermind of the German Army, General Ludendorff, called 'Der schwarze Tag' (the Black Day) of the German Army. With the Canadians on the right and in a line comprising British and French troops, the Australians achieved many victories between 8 August and 4 October 1918, the date of the last battle fought by the Corps, at Montbrehain.

Exploitation of the turning point achieved by John Monash brought about a series of spectacular victories. Sadly, more Australian lives were lost and the Australian battalions were reduced to the strength of companies, but after Hamel a triumphant end was always in sight.

Postscript

On 13 May 1918 Signaller Peter Hodge, of the First Australian Divisional Signal Company, heard by telegram that his brother Stan, a gunner, had died of wounds in No. 2 Australian Hospital, Boulogne, on 5 May. On 13 May he wrote in his diary:

The telegram knocked me all of a heap. I cannot realize that Stan has made the great sacrifice and given all for home and country. It is the best sacrifice, from which we can glean a certain amount of consolation. There is not a better way of leaving this world. But Stan has not left us but gone before. Humanity has three great consolations for the loss of one whom we held dear. To forget, to replace and to hope. But we cannot forget the one who has given his life for his country, we cannot replace a character that was of his nature irreplaceable, and to the materialist there is no hope.

Stan Hodge is buried in Boulogne Eastern Cemetery, Pas de Calais.

On 1 July 1919, Peter Hodge — who had served at Hamel — was on a troopship bringing Diggers home and it passed through Sydney Heads at 4 pm. Perhaps he had his diary in his hand because that very day he wrote: 'Before I went away I had an idea that Aussie was a good country but now I'm certain about it. It will do me to live and die in'. Peter returned to his home in Manly, NSW, and, much later, he died there.

He was fortunate: 60 000 other Diggers did not return to the 'good country'.

Appendix I: A Battalion Order for Battle

The 15th Battalion Order for the Battle of Hamel has survived, thanks to the efficient way in which the battalion war diary was kept by a succession of adjutants and intelligence officers. Secret in its time, this classic outline of an AIF battalion about to enter battle is worth readership by a wider audience than the officers for whom it was intended in 1918.

SecretCopy No. ......

15th Battalion Order. No. 45.

Reference Sheet 62 D, S.E. & S.W. 1/20,000

Vaux 1/20,000.

Battalion Headquarters,
2nd July, 1918.

1. GENERAL SCHEME
On a day and hour to be fixed, the 4th Brigade will capture Vaire and Hamel Woods, and consolidate on the spur East of those woods. Simultaneously the 6th Brigade on the right and the 11th Brigade on the left will capture and consolidate a line as shown on attached map.

2. TASKS
a. *The 15th Battalion*, plus G. Coy, of 132nd. American Regiment will attack on the North side of Vaire and Hamel Woods, with their final objective on the Blue line as shown on attached map.
b. *The 13th Battalion* will attack on the South side of Vaire Wood with final objective as shown on attached map.
c. *The 16th Battalion* will deal with Vaire Wood and Hamel Wood and then be withdrawn to original front line to act as a reserve Battalion.
d. *The 14th Battalion* will be a Reserve Battalion, and will carry and dump stores on a line approximately 500 yards in rear of Blue Line and then dig Support Line.

3. SPECIAL TASKS
a. *One Platoon* of C. Coy. under Lieut. Black will go forward immediately in

rear of last assaulting wave and dig a strong post in Support Line under supervision of engineers. Two Vickers Guns of 4th A.M.G. Coy. will go forward attached to this platoon.

b. The 15th Battalion will be responsible for mopping up the area marked blue on attached map. A. Coy will co-operate with three tanks for capturing 'Pear shaped' trench, moving on with rest of the line when this job is completed.

c. Two Sections of A. Coy. under Capt. J. P. G. Toft in conjunction with a party from 44th Battalion will form a liaison platoon to move along the inter Brigade boundary on the left. Capt. Toft will be responsible for keeping direction by compass bearing.

4. THE ATTACK

a. Jumping off line will be a taped line as shown on attached map, and Companies will form up on it in order from left to right, A.B.C.D. in four waves and advance in that formation.

b. Tape will be laid and Coy. frontages allotted on night of Y/Z.

5. MACHINE GUNS. Three Vickers guns will be attached to this Battalion. Two guns will go over with 'A' Coy. and one will move with 'D' Coy.

TRENCH MORTARS. Two trench mortars are allotted to this Battalion, and will move in rear of C. Coy.

TANKS will co-operate. Three at Pear shaped trench, three to right of it, and six along inter Brigade boundary. Instructions already issued as to guides Coys. will supply.

ARTILLERY

a. Artillery will put down normal harassing fire from Zero minus 8 minutes to Zero to drown noise of approaching tanks who will leave their forming up line 8 minutes before Zero.

b. Barrage will come down at Zero on the starting line shown on attached map, will remain thereon for four minutes and then advance by lifts of 100 yards at intervals of three minutes as shown on barrage map (to be issued later) to the 'Halt Line' shown on attached map, where there will be a pause of ten minutes. After the pause the barrage will lift 100 yards at intervals of four minutes up to four hundred yards beyond the blue line where it will remain.

c. On arrival at the 'Halt Line' a thick smoke screen will be built up to indicate the beginning of the ten minutes halt. Eight minutes afterwards a thick smoke screen will again be built up to indicate that the advance is about to be resumed.

d. After passing the Blue line the barrage will advance at a rate of one hundred yards in four minutes to a line four hundred yards beyond where it will continue as a standing barrage to cover consolidation for a period of thirty minutes.

6. WATCHES Watches will be synchronised at 9 P.M. and one hour before zero.

7. ACKNOWLEDGE

(Signed) .... Captain.
Adjutant 15th Battalion.

Distribution.

1. A. Company   4. D. Company
2. B. do   5. War Diary
3. C. do   6. File

Appendix II:
Battle of Hamel Board of Enquiry

On 18 November 1998, the Royal United Service Institution of New South Wales held a day-long seminar in Sydney to discuss all aspects of the Battle of Hamel. (RUSI had earlier carried out a similar exercise concerning the Battle of Fromelles.) Constituted as a Board of Enquiry, in the military style, the seminar was attended by hundreds of people, many of them with Service backgrounds. Members of RUSI 'acted' as John Monash, C. E. W. Bean, the artillery commander, the British Tank Corps commander, the German general involved and various other participants in the operation. The battle was subjected to close scrutiny under such themes as the plan, weather, topography, enemy, staff work, surprise and secrecy, assault troops, artillery and machine-gun support, communications, aircraft, tanks, US troops, flank brigades, exploitation and lessons. The President of the Board of Enquiry, Major General Gordon Maitland AO — who is also president of RUSI NSW — produced a summary of the Board's proceedings. One value of the battle, Maitland said, was that it showed that the Australian troops could operate successfully with Australian commanders and staff. Subject to meticulous preparation and staff work, the formidable German enemy was not invincible. Again, subject to planning and preparation, large-scale casualties could be avoided, while good morale and initiative at lower levels of command could overcome unforeseen difficulties or mitigate their effects.

The victory at Hamel, General Maitland stated, was measured not only by subjective values but also by objective and measurable yardsticks, in that:

- all objectives were taken and held;
- within the time allotted;
- with minimum casualties;
- by the employment of surprise;
- coupled with the use of technology; and

- thoroughly co-ordinated by efficient staff work and effective preparation.

In several instances the Board of Enquiry noted the quality of Monash's innovations — for example, in devising an order of march to the assault, follow-up and reserve troops so as to eliminate tiring marches.

Monash was eager to adopt new tactics, procedures and equipment, such as carrying stores by tanks, dropping ammunition by parachute, muffling the sound of tanks with aircraft noise, marking the front lines with flares, and using flexible platoon tactics during the assault. These progressive ideas gave confidence to the troops and helped to develop their feeling of invincibility and create high morale.

General Maitland said: 'The effective use of the Mark V tank was instrumental in the rapidity of the battle, effective consolidation through the supply tanks, ensuring a good reputation for the Tank Corps and continued employment of that Corps in all battles until the Armistice'.

The rapport and bonhomie between the US troops and the Australians could not be faulted, Maitland noted, and this good feeling between the armies bore fruit in the later months of the war as the Hindenburg Line was assaulted.

Speakers or 'performers' at the seminar pointed out that the Battle of Hamel was examined by higher HQs and in July 1918 GHQ [that is, Haig's GHQ for the entire British and Empire forces] distributed throughout the Army Staff Sheet 218 — 'Operations of the Australian Corps against Hamel'. The Board of Enquiry also had before it GHQ's further report, 'Notes on Recent Fighting, No 19'. (I have quoted from this report in my book.)

The Board found that while the Battle of Hamel was not one of the major operations of the war, it was decisive. 'It redressed and had significant influence upon the morale of the Allied forces and the general ethos of future operations during the next four months. The Battle of Hamel was a great success because all the component parts fitted well together and no major catastrophes occurred to blight the operation.'

The RUSI Board of Enquiry then assessed Hamel as 'decisive'. It raised Allied morale and GHQ (which in effect meant Haig himself) had recognised it as a major triumph.

I see the RUSI Board of Enquiry as significant in itself because it heightens Australian awareness of an operation which had been relatively obscure for generations.

The ladies and gentlemen of RUSI, all of whom are well informed — some of them are military historians in their own right — would be astonished to know that anybody purporting to be a specialist historian on the First World War could write a book devoted to the victory in 1918, yet suppress all mention of that turning-point battle. Some will view it as another deliberate attempt to downgrade Australian achievements.

Appendix III: Rewriting History

In the 1990s, British authors were making strenuous attempts, some of them ludicrous, to rewrite military history, especially in circumstances where Australians were involved. For instance, Rawlinson's biographer, F. Maurice, writes: 'The first of Rawlinson's victories was a fairly minor affair, an attack by two brigades to straighten out the line held by the Australian Corps'.

In that Rawlinson was Monash's Army commander, Hamel could be said to be within his responsibility, but to describe it as a 'Rawlinson victory' is absurd. To label it a 'fairly minor affair' is acceptable in relation to the gigantic battles that had preceded it but, if it was indeed 'minor', why was it acclaimed throughout the Allied political and military world? Would Clemenceau have left an important Allied conference in Versailles to bestow praise on the AIF and its commander? Monash was the recipient of the many compliments, not Rawlinson.

The most ridiculous, blatant and downright untrue version of Hamel appears in *Dictionary of World War I*, by Ian Hogg and published by Hutchinson under its Brockhampton Press imprint in 1994. Hogg writes:

Hamel, Capture of operation, July 1918. On 4 July 1918 the 33rd Illinois National Guard Division decided to celebrate Independence Day by attacking Hamel Wood, near Corbie on the Somme. In co-operation with some Australian troops, and after a severe artillery preparation, the combined force advanced under cover of tanks on a 6 km/4 mi front, the US forces concentrating on Hamel. The joint force advanced 2.5 km/1.5 mi. Hamel and Vaire Woods were taken, and 1500 prisoners, twenty mortars and 100 machine-guns were captured.

Since Mr Hogg is a veteran military historian of many admirable books, I have to wonder if his account of Hamel deliberately downgrades the Australian role. The major 'errors':

- The 33rd Illinois National Guard Division 'decided' nothing. It was persuaded to lend some men for the assault; in the end just two companies of them took part.

- That the attack took place on American Independence Day was not an American decision. The date was chosen by Monash and Rawlinson. Monash was paying the Americans a compliment.
- 'Some' Australian troops co-operated in the operation, according to Hogg. Australian officers did all the planning, with the able help of the senior British Tank Corps officers. Hogg does not mention the Tank Corps, the Royal Air Force, the Australian Flying Corps or units of the Royal Artillery. For him, Hamel was an American operation. The fact is, fewer than 1000 Americans took part, assisting 7500 Australians.
- Hogg states that the Americans 'concentrated' on Hamel; this is not so. The Australian battalions advanced on Hamel village with a few American platoons attached.

Monash has no entry in Hogg's *Dictionary*, though General Currie, commanding the Canadians Corps, does. Similarly, the Australian Imperial Force receives no entry, but then neither do the Canadians, other than in a list of British Commonwealth Forces. South Africa is said in this entry to have raised a force of 375 000. In fact, South Africa could supply only one brigade — though a very fine one. Exactly 76 184 South Africans went to the war. We are told that Amiens is an 'ancient city in NE France'. Ancient, yes, but in north-west France.

In 1998, to mark the anniversary of the end of the war, the Imperial War Museum, London, published *The Imperial War Museum Book of 1918 Year of Victory*. The author, Malcolm Brown, is an experienced historian and the IWM co-published his book with Sidgwick & Jackson, a leading firm. With this background it is an important book, virtually an official one since it is endorsed by the prestigious IWM. The focus is intended to be intense, concentrating on the final year of the war which, it is emphasised, was the year of victory.

After this, it is a matter of amazement that the Battle of Hamel, a notable victory, does not rate a mention, not even as a footnote or as a place-name. Hamel was a non-happening. John Monash is given three mentions: his description of the opening day of the Battle of Amiens, 8

August 1918; a brief reference to operations on 29 September; and his capable handling of the soldiers' repatriation after the war.

Mont St Quentin is mentioned though devoid of reference to Monash. Brown refers to the Digger statue on the slopes the Australians conquered, though his description of the soldier is odd. He writes of 'the sturdy figure of an Australian soldier in his distinctive swept-back cap'. This strange headgear may puzzle Australians who have not seen the statue; I can assure them that the 'swept-back cap' is actually the standard felt slouch hat with its left side turned up.

What is indicated by Malcolm Brown's omission of the Battle of Hamel in a book that stresses victory? Only he and his sponsors at the IWM can answer that question but they must not be surprised if Australians see it as yet another attempt to rewrite history, this time by the shrewd device of not writing anything about certain events. It is, in effect, a form of censorship.

Brown records interesting observations about the Diggers. The most graphic description of all comes in a letter written by Lieutenant Philip Ledward of the British 8th Division, and which Brown quotes. In part, the letter reads, 'It is my considered opinion that the Australians, in 1918, were better in a battle then any troops of either side. They were not popular. They had a contempt for Britishers to begin with ... I myself heard the expression 'not bad for a Britisher' used by one about a successful feat of British arms. They were untidy, undisciplined, 'cocky' ... but it seems to me indisputable that a greater number of them were personally indomitable, in the true sense of the word, than any race. I am glad they were on our side'. The Digger who uttered the words 'not bad for a Britisher' was not being contemptuous but truly complimentary, but how could the English Lieutenant Ledward be expected to understand the unique subtleties of Digger language? The soldier might equally have said, 'Not bad for a Kiwi' or a 'Canadian' or a 'Tasmanian'; it was his way of expressing admiration.

Another British military historian, Robin Neillands, produced an 80th anniversary book, *The Great War Generals 1914–1918*. This superbly written book, brought out by Robinson Publishing, deals fairly with Monash and his Hamel victory. Nevertheless, Neillands is on the defensive and feels it necessary to cover himself against possible Australian criticism. He writes: 'Lest any Australian historian or critic should take offence at this brief overview of General Monash and taking offence is something that they can be all too eager to do, let it be noted that not I, nor anyone consulted in the course of researching and writing this book, has anything but the earnest praise for General Monash and the splendid troops he had the honour to command. The only point I would make, however, is that the British troops from the United Kingdom also performed well, did their share of the fighting, for longer, and suffered far and away the bulk of the casualties, a small acknowledgment of that fact from time to time might not go amiss'.

I make such acknowledgment here. Most Australians had and still have great respect for the United Kingdom troops and are well aware of their service and sacrifice in the First World War. Who could possibly dispute what Robin Neillands writes? Certainly not this military historian. However, Australians draw a sharp distinction between the UK troops together with their junior leaders and some of the senior commanders, notably Haig, Rawlinson, Gough and Haking; — and French, though he never commanded Australian troops. The Australians, incidentally, were not the only troops wasted by Gough; the Canadians, by autumn 1917, even refused to serve under him.

Rawlinson, though being thoroughly disliked by Australian historians, nevertheless gets favourable mention from those who know that almost alone among the higher commanders he opposed capital punishment. It is interesting that Rawlinson presented a number of Australian officers with a copy of Kipling's famous poem, 'If', and ordered them to learn it and 'think it over'. The poem is by a father to his son, listing all the qualities which, if he can develop them, will assure him of success and make a man of him.

Australians are sensitive concerning ill-informed slights about the Diggers and especially when they are misrepresented and ignored. Acknowledgment of victories such as that at Hamel 'from time to time might not go amiss', to quote Robin Neillands. Indeed, he makes due acknowledgment, Malcolm Brown does not. The stark difference in approach to the Australians between Neillands and Brown is quite remarkable.

Canadians, too, deserve more credit than they receive from most British military writers. This is especially so in the case of Lieutenant-General Sir Arthur Currie, who commanded the Canadian troops from April 1917 to the end of the war. While he is one of the least well known senior commanders, one British historian, Denis Winter, considers him to be 'the most successful Allied general'. Winter says, in his controversial book, *Haig's Command*, 'Currie's capture of the Drocourt-Queant Switch in autumn 1918 remains the British Army's greatest achievement on the Western Front'. Currie stated in his diary, 'Thorough preparation must lead to success. Neglect nothing'. In this he was like Monash.

Poor General Currie — he does not rate a mention in Malcolm Brown's index to his 385-page book on 1918; Drocourt-Queant Switch is covered in four lines. Currie is a non-general as Hamel is a non-battle.

Appendix IV
'Ninety-Three Minutes in the History of the World'

At the dedication of the Australian Corps Memorial Park, Le Hamel, on 4 July 1998, the Australian Minister for Veterans' Affairs, The Hon. Bruce Scott MP, gave an address which admirably and concisely expressed the significance of the Battle of Hamel and of the new Australian Corps Memorial Park.

I know all of us here today share the belief that commemoration of the past is a key to understanding ourselves and the world around us.

That there are essential human truths, as constant as nature itself, which ignore time.

The Battle of Hamel, although only ninety-three minutes in the history of the world, proved many of these truths.

And here, eighty years after the tank engines roared and young soldiers moved off towards the battleline, we return to honour the men of the Australian Corps and the lessons they made clear.

Le Hamel proved that, amid uncertainty and possible defeat, a spark — although small — can be struck by determined, well-led men.

And from that flicker, a blaze can be fanned into life. Hamel was such a spark, a turning point — for behind it lay the great German assaults of March and April when the whole Allied line seemed set to shatter, but in desperation held together. Ahead, the German army's 'Schwarzer Tag', their 'Black Day' and then the months of Allied success until final victory in November.

Hamel told an exhausted and war weary world to hold on.

It proved that, in war or peace, all life is precious and success is ultimately the prize of any leader committed to preserving it and its dignity.

Monash, an Australian commanding Australians, his tactics so painstakingly crafted to limit casualties, was such a man. His name is well known in our homeland, universities and suburbs carry it in honour of him.

But better than all these accolades, are the hundreds, if not thousands of young Australians alive today because their grandfathers or great grandfathers served under his command.

My own great uncle, Ken Bassett of the 15th Battalion served here at this place. He had survived Pozières, Bullecourt, Passchendaele and Villers-Bretonneux by his own skill and courage and, one must suppose, sheer luck. At Hamel, he also had Monash.

In another of life's great lessons, Monash proved that using men's minds as well as their bodies, trusting their intellect and initiative, would achieve results.

No longer cannon fodder, sheep driven into the bloody slaughter of years past, but free men, partners in the enterprise before them. In the fight for France's liberty, equality and fraternity found new form at Hamel.

We found new friends also. Today, we recognise the contribution of American soldiers, who advanced in their first offensive operation of the First World War.

And we recognise the role of British Armour and French artillery.

The operation in itself, a microcosm of those nations who have formed the great solid coalition for peace and freedom throughout this long and battle-scarred century.

This Memorial, sited on an original trench, will eternally record not just the deeds of those who fought the Battle of Hamel, but indeed all those who served in the five divisions of the Australian Corps.

The images sandblasted into these walls of Australian granite will tell those who come here of the big-hearted Australians and their determination — shared by all the allied forces — to see aggression defeated and liberty defended.

Many, many people have devoted their time and energy to this project and the magnificent end result is a tribute to their enthusiasm. We are of course especially indebted to those who provided the land on which the Park is now built.

In addition, I would like to particularly acknowledge the work of Dr John Laffin, who has believed in this project and many others on the

Western Front for more than forty years. I hope, John, that you are as proud of the result as I am.

This Memorial will stand as a reminder to future generations of many things.

Loss and sacrifice certainly.

For although a great success in contemporary terms, we mourn the loss and suffering of 1400 young Australian men wounded or killed here.

As a memorial to courage.

The courage of individuals like Tom Axford of Kalgoorlie and Henry Dalziel from Irvinebank, both recipients of the Victoria Cross for the part they played in the battle.

The courage of countless other diggers — men like Eric Abraham, Howard Pope, Charles Mance and Ted Smout — as they braved shell and machine-gun fire in reaching and then clearing the German lines.

The courage of men like Monash and his senior commanders who risked failure with new and untried tactics.

And it will stand as a monument to the power of new technologies and the older power of the human spirit. Its capacity for determination, and creativity and friendship.

Its capacity to disregard the past and set itself upon a new and better path towards victory.

All these things we commemorate with this Memorial — built not just with granite and steel, but on the deep, committed friendship which endures and thrives between the people of France and Australia.

Together we will ensure that the lessons, the truths of eighty years ago and of today, are passed on beyond our own time and into the bright gleaming future, secured with such determination and valour by the men of the Australian Corps.

Glossary

ACK EMMA: the morning (from am in phonetic alphabet)

AID POST: synonymous with the RAP as the nearest medical post to the firing line

AMMO: universal British and Empire term for ammunition, especially SAA (see abbreviations)

ARCHIE: anti-aircraft fire

BATTLE ORDER: infantry equipment reduced to the essentials with the pack removed and replaced with the haversack

BILLJIM: Australian soldiers' term for themselves

BOMB: frequently used in the 1914–18 war as the term hand grenade

BREASTWORK: a 'trench' built above wet or marshy ground; the front and rear walls were made of loose earth, sandbags, tree trunks and branches, masonry, smashed furniture and anything else available

BULLRING: training ground where recruits and convalescents were drilled for service at the front

CADRE: selected officers and men held back when a battle went into action, on whom the unit was built in the event of heavy casualties. Also known as LOB men (left out of battle)

CASE-SHOT: artillery shell for anti-personnel use; filled with steel balls, pellets, chain links

CHATS: Australian term for lice, which infested all front-line soldiers

CHIT: any note or written message

COAL-BOX: shell-burst causing a cloud of black smoke

COMMUNICATION TRENCH: any trench dug at an angle to the fighting trench and along which men and supplies moved

DAISYCUTTER: a shell that exploded immediately on contact with the ground; very dangerous for infantry advancing

DEMONSTRATION: a feint attack or bombardment

DIGGER: an Australian or New Zealand soldier

DINKUM: Australian for good, true, authentic; a Gallipoli veteran was a 'dinkum'; 'dinkum oil' was authenticated news

DON R: dispatch rider (from phonetic alphabet of signalese)

DOUGHBOY: nickname for American troops, which they preferred to Yank or Sammy

DUCKBOARDS: wooden planking in muddy trenches or across muddy ground; without duckboards the armies would have been virtually immobile

DUD: a shell failing to explode; or anything else that was considered useless

EGG GRENADE: small German egg-shaped grenade

ENFILADE, TO: to fire along a trench from the end; not synonymous with flanking fire

FASCINE: bundle of brushwood carried on tanks to fill trenches and ditches to enable them to cross

FIELD DRESSING: small pouch of bandage and iodine carried by each soldier for application to a wound of his own

FIRE BAY: that part of the trench manned by the troops ready to repel an attack

FIRE STEP: the step on the forward side of a trench upon which soldiers stood to observe or fire; the step was upwards from the trench floor

FIVE-NINE: British term for a 5.9-inch German shell

FRITZ: the troops' general name for Germans; a diminutive of Friedrich

GREENCROSS: German gas shell; a reference to the mark painted on the shell

GS: General service, such as GS wagon

HEINIE: American troops' slang for a German

HELIOGRAPH: a signalling instrument, using sunflashes to send morse code

HOP THE BAGS: leap over the parapet for move forward to the attack; also a hop-over

HOWITZER: a gun with a high, lobbing trajectory for shelling trenches and landing its shells behind enemy cover

HUN: Digger slang for German

IDENTITY DISC: The name-tag bearing the soldier's number unit and religion. From 1916–17 Diggers wore two. No. 1, green, remained on the dead soldier to identify the corpse for reburial; No. 2, the red, was removed at the time of the original burial as proof of death; Australians called them dead-meat tickets; they were never known as dog-tags

JACK JOHNSON: type of German shell that burst with a loud report and black smoke

JACKS: the hateful term for military police

JERRY: another term for a German soldier

KAMERAD: (1)literally, comrade or mate; (2) the cry by Germans wanting to surrender

LIFTING BARRAGE: gunfire that advanced in range, according to a predetermined timetable

LINE: usually the front line or firing line

LISTENING POST: a dangerously advanced post, usually in No-Man's-Land, where two or three soldiers listened at night for sounds of enemy movement

MINENWERFER: German trench mortar, often referred to as a minnie

MOP-UP: when infantry moved through enemy trenches some soldiers were left to 'mop up' any enemy troops still in dugouts or trenches

ORDERLY: soldier detailed for special duty

OVER THE TOP: to go over the parapet in an attack

PARADOS: the rear side of a trench

PARAPET: the side of the trench facing the enemy

PICKET: (1)barbed wire supporting stake; (2) patrol or sentry

PILLBOX: concrete post to protect crew of an MG

POSSIE: Australian for 'position' and much used among Diggers

PUSH: an attack in great strength, an offensive

REDOUBT: strong point in the trench system

RUM JAR: term for German mortar bomb, because of its shape

RUNNER: soldier carrying messages

SALIENT: any trench system protruding into the enemy's defensive system

SANDBAG: sack filled with earth; trench defences were built from sandbags

SAP: narrow trench, usually for penetration into No-Man's-Land

SHRAPNEL: lead or steel balls packed into a shell case from which they were ejected at high velocity about five metres above the ground; shards and splinters from HE shells were not shrapnel

START LINE: the white-tape line marking the jumping-off place

STUNT: Digger term used to describe any attack, raid or action

STRAFE: a hail of fire or bombardment

TOFFEE APPLE: large spherical mortar bomb with firing shaft attached

TRACER: phosphorescent machine-gun bullet which glowed in flight; one tracer was used for every seven ordinary rounds and it gave a clear indication of the aim

TRAVERSE: angle in a trench that limited the effect of enfilade fire or shell-burst

VERY: the ubiquitous signal of illuminating flare, fired from a Very pistol, named after the inventor, E. W. Very

WALKING WOUNDED: men wounded but, with wounds dressed, able to walk to the rear for further attention

WHIPPET: a particular light tank and then, from usage, any light tank

WHIZZBANG: a high-velocity, low-trajectory shell that made a shrill approach noise and then a sharp explosive report

Z: for Zero hour, the time that an attack commenced

General Index

- *Ranks of individuals changed during course of War; ranks recorded here are usually ranks at time of events covered in this text.*
- *Battles are listed under place names in this Index.*
- *Battalions, divisions etc. are listed in a separate Index.*

Abraham, Eric 164
Accroche Wood 56, 70 (map), 71, 95, 99, 147–8
Akeroyd, Capt. G. W. 90
Adams, Capt. E. C. 96
Ailette 100
Aire 27
Aisne & Aisne River 11, 21, 62
Albert 6 (map), 14, 49, 88, 90, 92, 98
Allonville 66
Amiens 6 (map), 56, 59, 69, 70 (map), 71, 103, 144, 158–9
Ancre River 14, 89, 91, 92, 95
Anderson, Colin (stonemason) 148
Anderson, Private D. J. 77
Ardennes, Battle of 20
Armentières 27, 28, 29
Arras 48
Artois 21
Aubers Ridge 21, 35, 36, 37, 41
Aubigny 66
Australian Corps Memorial Park (Hamel)
Battlefield Tour 143–9
Clemenceau's words 126
description of Park 148–9
development of 8, 14–16, 143
Feint Attack North Somme recognition 87
Laffin's role in 8, 14–16, 143, 163–4
opening/dedication of 16, 162–4
Scott, Bruce 8, 15, 16
Australian Imperial Force (AIF)
see individual person and place names; see other Index for battalions, divisions etc.
Axford, Lance Cpl Thomas VC 79, 147, 164

Barnes, Geoff (film director) 143
Bassett, Ken 163
battles *see individual place names*
Beaumont-Hamel 13–14
Bean, C. E. W. (author)

11th Brigade, B on 131
Clemenceau visit, B. on 126
Fromelles battle, B on 39
Hamel, B. on 57, 71, 80, 81, 101, 111, 113, 117, 137, 154
Hughes, B's 'kernel' of message to troops 129
Laffin's assessment of B's work 8, 9
Official History 8, 71, 113, 137
Pozières battle, B. on 44
Beaverbrook, Lord 14
Belfort 11
Bell, Maj. Gen. George (US) 65, 129–30
Bellenglise 14
Bethune, Lt F. B. 26
Bingham, Colonel D. 80
Birdwood, Lt Gen. Sir William
Australian Corps GOC 26, 31, 37, 47, 52, 53, 128, 140
Australian transfer to Western Front 26
Bullecourt tank offensive 47–8
Gallipoli 26, 31, 45
Haig comment to B. re Turks 45
Irvine's raid, B's praise for 52
Monash and B. 53, 128, 140
promoted to command 5th Army 52–3
superior officers, relationship with 45–6, 47–8, 49, 54
White (Brudenell White) relationship 37, 45–6, 53
Blamey, Brigadier T. A. 53, 56, 60, 69
Blee, Lieutenant H. E. 102
Blinman, Sgt Major H. G. 79, 102
Boar's Head Salient 35
Bois Grenier 29
Boulogne 150
Bouzencourt 70 (map)
Brand, Brigadier C. H. 47, 48, 49
Brewer, Private F. 102, 110, 112
Brick Beacon 87, 89
Bridoux Salient 28

Broodseinde Ridge (Passchendaele), Battle of 50
Brook, Lieutenant F. R. 76
Brown, Malcolm (author) 158–9, 160, 161
Brudenell White, Brigadier/ Major General
see White, Major General Cyril Brudenell Bingham
Bullecourt
Australian losses at 48, 50
Battles of
First Battle of (April 1917) 15, 47–8, 67
Second Battle of (May 1917) 49–50
conference, lack of causing disaster 67
Dalziel VC at 86
Haig and 48, 49
reconnaissance (AIF) at 47
tank offensive at 47–8, 60, 61, 76, 107, 114, 115, 127
Bussy-les-Daours 104–5, 126
Butler, Lt General R. H. K. 51
Byng, General J. H. G. 140

Cambrai, Battle of 58, 65, 107, 114, 116
Campbell, Lieutenant W. E. 87
Canaway, Lieutenant R. A. 84
Cannan, Brigadier J. H. 131–4
Cantigny 118
Carter, Capt. E. K. 77
Central Copse (Hamel) 72, 147
Chadwick, Lieutenant L. 88
Champagne campaigns 21
Charleroi (Sambre), Battle of 20
Clemenceau, Georges (French PM) 5, 104–5, 126, 137, 157
Cochrane, Corporal H. S. 103
Conrad, Lieutenant Harry 101
Contay 45
Cook, Private L. A. 92
Cook, Sir Joseph (Aust. Min. Navy) 128–9
Cope, Capt. H. S. 77

Corbie 70 (map), 56, 106, 126, 157
Cornish, Lieutenant C. R. 96
Courage, Brigadier A. 57, 58, 60, 127
Coxen, Major General W. A. 58, 59, 60, 69
Craven, Lieutenant J. D. 102
Currie, Lt General Sir Arthur 158, 161

Daley, Lance Corporal M. J. 79
Dalziel, Private Henry (Harry) VC 77–8, 86, 146, 164
Daours Communal Cemetery Extension 103
Darke, Sergeant F. J. 75
Davies, Lieutenant J. E. 91
Davis, Colonel Abel (US) 9, 121
Dawson, Capt. F. C. 89, 91, 92
de Cary, General Fernand de Langle (Fr) 21
Degoutte, General Jean (French) 137
Delville Wood 14, 116
Dernancourt 98
Drake-Brockman, Lieutenant Colonel E. A. 127
Drocourt-Queant Switch 161
d'Urbal, General Victor 22
Dwyer, Lieutenant J. J. VC 138
Dwyer, Lieutenant T. 81

Egypt 25, 26, 30
El Alamein 17
Elles, Major General Hugh 56, 58, 114–5, 118, 127
Elliott, Brigadier H. E. ('Pompey') 40, 52, 87–93, 98 see also Feint Attack North of Somme
Emerson, Lieutenant E. K. (US) 120
Eu 120

Facey, Lieutenant S. G. 90
Falkenhayn see von Falkenhayn
Feint Attack North of Somme 87–93
  Brick Beacon 87, 89
  casualties 88, 90, 93, 113
  Elliott's tactics 87, 88–9
  'friendly fire' 113
  Germans and 87, 88, 90, 91, 92–3, 98
  Gill, Signaller G. T. 113
  Hamel, significance of feint attack 87, 93

  objectives and achievements 87, 93
  papier-mâché dummies 87
  prisoners 88
  recognition in memorial park 87
  Sailly-Laurette 87
  significance of in Hamel success 87
  timing of 87, 89–90
First World War (prior Hamel) see also person & place names
  Allied reaction to 18–19, 24
  Australian reaction to 18–19, 24, 63
  battles
    of 1914–15 19–24
    other battles see individual place names
  early expectations of 18
  Kitchener's reappraisal of 22–3
  losses (overall) 18, 23
  mechanisation 24
  movement of troops 24
  railways 24
  Schlieffen Plan 19
  tactics (general) 22–4
  trench warfare, beginnings of 23
Fisher, Andrew (Aust. politician) 19, 24
Fleming, Lieutenant J. H. 91
Flers 107, 116
Fleurbaix 27, 36, 39
Flintoft, Lieutenant W. 91, 92
Floyd, Private D. W. 103
Foch, General/Marshal Ferdinand (French) 20, 126
Foss, Captain Maitland 28–9
Franvillers Communal Cemetery Extension 88
French, General Sir John 21, 25, 33, 160
Fromelles 33–43
  Battle of 15, 32, 33–43
  'Board of Enquiry' 154
  daylight attack failure 88
  Elliott at 40, 88
  failure, reasons for 40–1
  'friendly fire' 113
  Haig and 33, 35, 36, 37, 41, 42
  Haking and 33–43, 44
  Somme, relation to 33, 35, 36, 37, 38, 41
  unilateral change of plan 67
Frontiers of France, Battle of 19–20
Fuller, Lieutenant Colonel J. F. C. 56, 57, 58

Gale, Capt. C. M. (US) 119, 120–1
Gallipoli 11, 19, 25, 26, 27, 28, 31, 45, 50, 86, 105, 138, 166
Gaze, Lieutenant F. O. 96
Gellibrand, Brigadier/Major General John 49–50, 53
George V 42, 127, 140
Gibbs, Philip (war correspondent) 121–3
Gill, Signaller G. T. 85, 113
Glasgow, Brigadier/Major General T. W. 51–2, 53, 105, 138
Gough, General, Sir Hubert 46, 47–8, 49, 53, 160
Grogan, Brigadier G. W. St G, VC 51
Guedeccourt 86
Gussing, Private H. E. 107–8

Hagan, Capt. Robert G. (US) 120
Haig, General/Field Marshal Sir Douglas
  American troops at Hamel 65, 68–9, 124, 130
  Australians, H's assessment of 45–6
  Bullecourt 48, 49
  French leaders, H's attitude to 137
  French (Sir John) replaced by Haig 25
  Fromelles, Battle of 33, 35, 36, 37, 41, 42
  Gallipoli, disparaging remark re 45
  George V relationship 42, 140
  GHQ 35, 42, 57, 115, 127, 135–6, 138, 142, 155
  Haig's Command (book) 142, 161
  Haking relationship 33, 35, 36, 37, 41, 42
  Hamel and H. 60, 63, 135–6, 137, 155
  Hindenburg Line, H's comment on capture of 49
  Laffin misgivings re H. 160
  Loos, Battle of 22
  Monash and H. 69, 127, 138, 139, 140
  Neuve-Chapelle, Battle of 21
  Pozières, H's assessment of 45–6
  Rawlinson, and American troops at Hamel 68–9, 130
  Somme offensive 30–1, 45–6
  Supreme War Council (Versailles) 126

tanks 115, 116
Turks, opinion of by H. 45
Villers-Bretonneux 51
Haking, Lieutenant General Sir Richard 33–43, 44, 160
Hale, Staff Captain 13
Hamel (Village & Battle of) see also Feint Attack North of Somme
    aircraft use of 59, 62, 63, 64, 66, 73, 95, 99, 104, 107, 124–5, 135, 141
    Americans and 16, 65–9, 72, 74, 75, 83, 107, 112, 118–24, 129–30, 132, 155, 157–8, 163
    ammunition carriers & drops 62, 63, 125, 147, 148
    artillery at 56, 58–65, 69, 73–5, 80, 84, 85, 95–8, 117, 133, 135, 136, 145, 152–3, 154, 157–8, 163
    'Board of Enquiry' 154–6
    British and 60, 90, 95, 163
    casualties 72, 75, 77, 78, 79, 83, 97, 99, 102–6, 107–13
    communications 62–3, 80, 131
    criticisms of Hamel 130–4
    date of battle 12, 73, 157–8
    discoveries by author at site 12–15
    diversionary attack 64
    duration of battle 16, 85, 162–4
    enemy weapons used by AIF 136
    exploitation of success (tactics of) 132
    Feint Attack North of the Somme 87–93
    film about battle 15, 143
    French artillery 163
    'friendly fire' 61, 75, 96, 113
    front, length of 59–60, 157
    gas 12, 73, 74, 80, 82, 86, 96, 112
    Germans at
        counterattack 86, 94–100
        defences 55, 66, 71–3, 74, 77, 79, 80, 81, 82, 83, 98–9, 112, 122, 136, 145, 164
        histories & assessments 98–9
        HQ (Wolfsberg) 70 (map), 95, 99, 148
    Haig and 60, 63, 135–6, 137, 155
    historical recognition of battle 156, 157–61

Huns Walk 98, 103, 117, 147
    infantry skill & spirit 135–6
    intelligence 66, 73–4, 83, 100
    IWM Book of 1918, no entry 158
    Kidney Trench 79, 146–7
    manpower 63–5, 85, 1328
    map 6, 70
    materials captured 97
    medical supplies 110
    memorial see Australian Corps Memorial Park
    message maps 59
    Monash and see Monash–Hamel
    morale and Hamel 120, 126, 127, 128, 136, 154, 155
    'Moran's House' 83–4
    mortars 78, 82, 96, 97, 147, 157
    name of village 17
    Pear Trench 70 (map), 75, 77, 78, 81, 99, 105, 109, 113, 117, 138, 143, 145–6, 152
    'peaceful penetration' nearby 52
    phosphorus bomb 79
    Pioneer Switch Trench 105
    plans, initial & amended 60
    pontoon bridge 73
    Pozières, lessons from 59
    prisoners, German 71, 76, 83, 84, 97, 98, 99, 101, 102, 103, 119, 120–1, 147, 157
    raids after battle 98
    Rawlinson and 55, 60, 128, 157, 158
    reconnaissance 59, 62, 63, 66, 73, 81, 83, 95, 124–5, 132, 134, 141
    salient spur 55, 56, 57, 95
    Scott speech re 162–4
    secrecy & deception 59, 66–7, 73, 74, 80, 100, 135–6
    significance of see Hamel–success
    souvenir hunters 101, 119
    success, analysis of 17, 135–42, 149, 154–6, 164
    tactics & strategy of battle 16, 17, 55–69, 73, 80–1, 98–100, 101, 131–4, 135–6, 139–42, 161–4
    tanks at 56–7, 58, 60, 61, 64, 65, 71, 74, 75–6, 77, 80–3, 98–9, 102, 107, 108, 114–18, 127, 131, 135–6, 138, 145, 147–8, 152, 155, 158

terrain 55, 57, 66, 71, 72, 95
    trenches at 12–15, 55, 71, 75, 77, 78, 79, 80, 81, 96, 97, 99, 105, 109, 112, 117, 138, 143, 145, 146, 147, 148, 152, 163
    village 54–5
    Villers-Bretonneux and 55, 56, 57, 95, 97
    wounded evacuation 107–10
Hamel Wood 66, 70 (map), 78, 79, 99, 146, 151, 157
Hamelet 145
Harbonnières, Heath Cemetery 101
Harper, Captain G. 81
Hébuterne 84
Heggen, Air Vice-Marshal Alan 8, 15
Henderson, Captain R. J. 50
Heneker, General Sir G. W. G. 51, 52
Heritage, Captain K. 29
Hindenburg Line 14, 15, 47–50, 155
Hobbs, Major General Joseph 89
Hodge, Gunner Stan 150
Hodge, Signaller Peter 150
Hogg, Ian (author) 157–8
Holmes, Major General W. 47
Howard, John (Aust. PM) 8
Hughes, W. M. (Aust. PM) 63, 126, 128–9
Hunn, Major S. A. 66–7, 83
Huns Walk 98, 103, 117, 147
Hutchinson, Sergeant W. P. 91

Ibbotson, Corporal A. 90
Ieper see Ypres
Irvine, Lieutenant A. W. 52

Jackson, Private William VC 29–30
Jacob, Lt General Sir Claud 140
Joffre, Gen. Joseph-Jacques-Césaire (Fr) 21
Kidney Trench (Hamel) 79, 146–7
King George V 42, 127, 140
Kipling, Rudyard (author) 160
Kitchener, Lord (Horatio) Herbert 22–3

La Bassée 20
Laffin, Hazelle 8, 11, 14
Laffin, John (author) 8–9, 11, 12–16, 143, 163–4

Lagnicourt 86
Lamotte-Warfusée (map) 70
Landon, Captain Philip 42
Le Cateau, Battle of 20, 21
Le (or le) Hamel *see* Hamel
Le Verguier 84
Ledward, Lieutenant Philip 159
Liddell Hart, Capt. Basil H. (author) 9, 139
Lihou, Sergeant James Victor 84–5
Lille 30, 36, 41
Little, Sergeant P. L. 91
Lloyd George, David (British PM) 126, 139–40
Loos 21–2, 25, 35
Lorraine, Battle of 20
Lusitania (ship) 122
Lutyens, Sir Edwin 14
Lynch, Private J. J. 96–7
Lys Sector & Battle 52, 62

MacLagen *see* Sinclair-MacLagen
Maitland, Major General Gordon AO 154, 155
Mallon, Capt. G. H. (US) 78
Mance, Charles 164
Mangin, General Charles (French) 57, 137
Mann, Lieutenant A. W. 50–1
Marcelcave 70 (map)
Marks, Lieutenant Colonel D. G. 59, 127
Marne River, First Battle of 20–1
Marseilles 27
Masoner, Capt. W. J. (US) 119
Maurice, F. (author) 157
Maxse, General Sir Ivor 140
McCay, Major General James Whiteside 36, 39, 40
McDonald, Capt. K. G. 90, 92
McLachlan, Ian (Aust. Minister Defence) 16
McPherson, Lieutenant W. J. 90
McPhie, CSM A. E. 92
McSharry, Lt Colonel T. P. 78, 105–6, 109, 127
Menin Road 50
Menzies, Sir Robert (Aust. PM) 15
Méricourt-l'Abbé Communal Cemetery Extension 90, 93
Messines 15, 50, 86
Minchin, Lieutenant J. B. 79
Moltke, General Helmuth (German) 21

Monash, Lieutenant General Sir John
aircraft, use of 59, 62, 63, 64, 73, 135, 141
analysis of success 135–42
artillery and 58–60, 64, 73, 135, 140, 141
assessments of M. 138, 139–40, 140–2
Australian Corps Memorial Park and 16
Australian publicity of success 128, 141
biographies of 8, 9
Birdwood and 53, 128, 140
Blamey, M's appt of 53
'Board of Enquiry' 154
casualties, views on 63–4, 163
Clemenceau visit to M. 126
command, size of 140–1
commander AIF 3rd Div. 50, 53
communications 62–3
congratulations on success 126–30, 135–6, 157
criticisms of Hamel 130–4
failure to be promoted higher 140
Feint Attack North of the Somme 89
GOC Aust. Corps (promotion) 52–3, 54
Haig and M 69, 127, 138, 139, 140
Haking, contrasted with M. 42
Hamel, Battle of (Monash and)
air photographs, use of 59, 62
aircraft, use of 59, 62, 63, 64, 73, 135, 141
American troops 65–6, 67–9
ammunition drops 62, 63, 125, 147, 148
artillery at 58–60, 64, 65, 73, 80, 135
communications 62–3, 80
conferences 60–1, 67
confidence 69, 85
date of battle 158
deviations from plan 138
diversionary attack 64
duration (of battle)
prediction 85
Feint Attack North of Somme 89
flares sighting 63
gas 73, 80
infantry & tanks 117, 135–6
infantry protection 64
intelligence 66, 73–4

manpower 63–5
message maps 59
M's own assessment of Hamel 136–7
motor cycles 62
plans, initial & amended 60
pontoon bridge 73
reconnaissance 63, 66, 73
secrecy & deception 59, 66–7, 73, 80, 135–6
subordinates, M's relationship with 60–1, 67, 69, 133, 138, 163
tactics at 17, 42, 55–69, 71, 73, 80, 98, 101, 133, 135–6, 139–40, 141–2, 161, 162–3, 164
tanks at 56–7, 58, 60, 64, 65, 71, 114, 117, 118, 135–6
turning point 149
Hogg's *Dictionary*, M. no entry 158
Hughes and M 63–4, 128
IWM Book of 1918, entries 158–9
infantry protection, M's views 64
inventiveness 139–40, 141–2, 155
Liddell Hart's assessment of M. 139
Lloyd George's assessment of M. 139–40
memoirs 17
Messines 50
Monash as a Military Commander (book) 128
Montgomery's assessment of M. 139
'musical score' (M's quote re battle plans) 69, 137
'peaceful penetration' 52
Pozières, M's lesson from 59
promoted to GOC Aust. Corps 52–3, 54
Rawlinson and M. 60, 68–9, 114, 128, 160
repatriation of soldiers 159
restriction on command 32
Rosenthal, M's support for 56
self-assessment 136–7, 141
Sixsmith's assessment of M. 140
statistical summary of corps achievements 141
subordinates, M's relationship with 60–1, 67, 69, 133, 138, 163
suburb named after 163

tactics 17, 42, 50, 55–69, 71, 73, 80, 98, 133, 135–6, 139–40, 141–2, 161, 162–3, 164
tanks, M's assessment of 56–7, 58, 61, 64, 114, 117, 118, 135–6
Taylor's assessment of M. 139
The Great War Generals 1914–1918, entry 159–60
ultimate responsibility taken by 67
war correspondents, M's relationship with 116–17
weakness in M's approach to battle 133
Winter's assessment of M. 142
Monro, General Sir Charles 36, 37
Mons 19–20, 21
Mont St Quentin 14, 15, 159
Montague, Sir Edwin 128
Montbrehain 149
Montgomery, Field Marshal Bernard and 17, 139
Montgomery, Major General A. A. 128
Monument Wood 70 (map), 82
Moore, Lieutenant John 93
Moran, Capt. J. T. 81–2, 83–4
'Moran's House' 83–4
Moreuil 118
Morlancourt 52, 56, 89, 95, 98
Mortimore, Capt. H. W. 116
Mouquet Farm 46, 81, 85
Murray, Captain Harry VC 81

Napoleon Bonaparte 18–19, 24, 35
Neillands, Robin (author) 159–60
Neuve-Chapelle 21, 35
Newfoundland 13–14, 24
Nieuport 11
Nord, *département of* 11
Notamel Wood 73, 81, 83, 102
'Nursery' (Western Front) 27, 30

O'Brien, Brigadier Kevin 8, 15, 143
Orlando, Vittorio (Italian PM) 126

Paris 126
Parrish, Joseph 103
Parrish, Private Thomas 103
Pas de Calais 103, 150
Passchendaele, Battle of 15, 50, 163

Pear Trench (Hamel) 70 (map), 75, 77, 78, 81, 99, 105, 109, 113, 117, 138, 143, 145–6, 152
Peden, Dr Peter (author) 8
Pedersen, P. A. (author) 57, 60–1, 128, 138, 140, 141
Péronne 6 (map), 14, 15, 70
Pershing, General John (US) 65, 67–8, 118, 126, 130
Pétain, General (French) 21
Piddington, Lieutenant W. T. 88
Pierregot 120
Plumer, General Sir Herbert 36, 50, 140
Polygon Wood 14, 50
Pope, Corporal Thomas (US) 124
Pope, Howard 164
Pozières 14, 15, 44–6, 48–9, 55, 59, 85, 163
Rabett, Lieutenant Colonel R. L. R. 48
Rainsford, Sergeant Bruce 99
Rawlinson, General Lord R. of Trent
American troops, use of 65, 68–9
anti-semitism of 128
biography 9, 157
capital punishment, opposition to 160
C-in-C India, R's ambition 128
Clemenceau visit 126
'education' of R. by Monash et al. 60
Haig, and use of American troops 68–9, 130
Hamel battle and 55, 60, 128, 157, 158
Handley Page bombers procured 63
Kipling's *If* (poem) 160
Laffin's comments re R. 160
Monash and R. 60, 68–9, 114, 127, 128, 140
tanks, R's opinion of 56–7, 114
Villers-Bretonneux 51
Raws, Lieutenant J. A. 45
Read, Major General G. W. (US) 65
Ribemont Communal Cemetery Extension 92
Rice, Bombadier G. M. 85–6
Rinkliff, Lieutenant F. L. (US) 66
Roach, Corporal Michael 75
Roberts, Lieutenant T. W. B. 102
Robertson, Brigadier J. C. 47, 48

Robertson, General Sir William 42
Rosenthal, Major General Charles 55–6
Ross Bastiaan plaque 148
Rule, Sergeant/Lieutenant E. J. 8, 45, 49, 71, 103–4, 118–9, 123
Ryan, Corporal T. 84
Ryan, Kate (film editor) 143

Sailly-le-Sec 14
Sailly-Laurette 56, 87
Sambre (Charleroi), Battle of 20
Sampson, Major/Colonel Burford 8, 72, 104–5, 113, 117, 126, 138
Sanborn, Colonel J. B. (US) 9, 66, 120
Sayers, Corporal D. A. 52
Scattergood, Lieutenant W. H. 90
Schram, Lieutenant Frank E. (US) 109–10, 124
Schulz, Lance Corporal B. V. 83
Scott, Bruce (Aust. Minister Vet. Affairs) 8, 15, 16, 162–4
Serle, Geoffrey (author) 9
Shaw, Corporal F. M. 76–7
Sinai Desert 11
Sinclair-MacLagan, Major General E. G.
Clemenceau visit 104, 126
commander 4th Division 56, 114, 128
credit for success 127–8
criticism by Cannan 134
Hamel and 60, 62, 63, 64, 65, 66, 101, 114
position before Hamel 56
Rawlinson's 'education' by S-MacL et al. 60
tanks and 56–7, 60, 114
Sixsmith, Major General E. K. G. 140
Skinner, Corporal E. C. 92
Smith-Dorrien, General 20
Smout, Ted 164
Smyth, Major General N. M. 49, 53
Soissons 118, 137
Somme 11, 14, 16, 30–1, 33, 35, 36, 37, 38, 41, 44–6, 52, 56, 66, 70, 73, 82, 87–93, 95, 100, 105, 147, 157,
Stafford, Lieutenant L. N. 88
Staples, Capt. W. J. 96

Stavely, Lieutenant W. C. B. 90–1
St Omer 27
Sugar Loaf salient 41
Symons, Lieutenant I. G. (US) 77

tanks
  Australian prejudice against
    60, 61, 62, 76, 114, 115,
    116, 127
  Bean and 57
  Birdwood and 47–8
  Blamey and 56, 60
  Bullecourt offensive failure
    47–8, 60, 61, 76, 107, 114,
    115, 127
  Cambrai 58, 107, 114, 116
  Courage and 57–8, 60, 127
  Coxen and 60
  Drake-Brockman and 127
  Elles and 56, 58, 114–5, 118,
    127
  Flers 107
  Fuller and 57, 58
  GHQ plans for 115, 127
  Gough and 47–8
  Haig and 115, 116
  Hamel, tanks at 56–7, 58, 60,
    61, 64, 65, 71, 74, 75–6, 77,
    80–3, 98–9, 102, 107, 108,
    114–18, 127, 131, 135–6,
    138, 145, 147–8, 152, 155,
    158
  Hamelet assembly of 145
  Liddell Hart book on 9
  Mangin's success with 57
  Marks and 127
  McSharry and 127
  Monash and 56–7, 58, 60, 61,
    64, 65, 114, 117, 118, 135–6
  Mortimore and 116
  Rawlinson 56–7, 114
  Sampson 117
  secrecy surrounding 58, 116
  Sinclair-MacLagen and 56–7,
    60, 114
  Soissons 137
  St Chamonds 118
  strategy & tactics 57–8, 60, 61,
    115, 117–8, 135
  Villers-Bretonneux 114
  vindication of 118, 127
  Western Front (general) 47–8
  White (Brudenell) and 47–8
Tasker, Lieutenant E. W. 91
Taylor, A. J. P. (author) 139
Taylor, D. M. (designer) 143
Terlicthun British Cemetery,
  Wimille 103

Thiepval 14, 44
Thompson, Lieutenant I. G.
  92, 93
Toft, Capt. J. P. G. 152
Transylvania (ship) 26
Tredenick, Lieutenant R. 52

Vaire-sous-Corbie 70, 74, 105,
  145
Vaire Trench (map) 70
Vaire Wood 66, 72, 78, 80–1,
  99, 100, 117, 122, 146, 147,
  151, 157
Vaux-en-Amienosis 61
Verdun, Battle of 22, 100
Versailles 126
Very, E. W. (light signal/pistol)
  95, 168
Victoria Crosses
  Axford, Lance Corporal Tom
    VC 79, 147, 164
  Dalziel, Private Henry VC 77–
    8, 86, 146, 164
  Dwyer, Lieutenant J. J. VC 138
  first AIF winner 29–30
  Jackson, Private William VC
    29–30
  Lihou, Sgt J. V. (deserving of
    VC) 84–5
  Shaw, Cpl M. W. (deserving
    of VC) 76–7
  Thompson, Lt I. G.
    (deserving of VC) 92, 93
  thousandth winner 85
  total number 30
  youngest 30
Ville-sur-Ancre 88, 89, 93, 97,
  98, 99
Villers-Bretonneux
  43rd Battalion casualties at 64
  Adelaide Cemetery 144
  artillery 51, 56
  Australian success 51
  Bassett survival 163
  Battlefield Tour 143, 144
  Battles of 15, 51, 64, 144
  Butler and 51
  château 144
  Crucifix Corner Cemetery 104
  Elliott and 52, 87
  gas at 64
  Glasgow and 51
  Grogan's comments on 51
  Haig and 51
  Hamel and V-B 55, 56, 57,
    95, 97
  Heneker and 51
  map 6, 70

military cemetery & memorial
  14, 75, 84, 88, 92, 96, 103,
  144–5
railway line 82
Rawlinson and 51
ridge 97
tanks at 114
Victoria School (Anzac
  Museum) 143, 144
Vimy Ridge 13, 14, 22
von Falkenhayn Erich (German
  chief-of-staff) 20, 21, 22
von Richthofen, Baron 148

Wagstaff, Brig./Maj.Gen. C. M.
  138–9
Walker, Major General H. B. 53
Watson, Major W. H. L. 47
Watts, Lieutenant L. S. 82
Western Front see place names
  and people
'White, Major General Cyril
  Brudenell Bingham
  Birdwood relationship 37, 45–
    6, 53
  'brilliant mind' 37, 45, 54
  Bullecourt tank offensive 47–8
  'courage & confidence' 114
  disputes with British
    commanders 37, 41, 45–6,
    47–8, 55
  Fromelles 37, 41
  Gallipoli 45
  Haig comment to BW re Turks
    45–6
  Hamel, initial views on 55
  Monash, BW seen as junior to
    53
  promoted Chief of Staff Fifth
    Army 53
  Pozières 45
Wilhelm, Crown Prince 22
Willis, Lieutenant H. D. 91
Wilson, Lt Gen./Gen. Sir
  Henry 42, 126
Winter, Denis (author) 142, 161
Wisdom, Brigadier E. A. 97, 99
Wolfsberg 70 (map), 95, 99,
  148
Wood, Lieutenant Ramsay 103–4
Woods, Capt. F. E. 79, 102,
  138
Wyllie, Capt. K. R. 87

Ypres 6 (map), 11, 14, 20, 35,
  46, 50, 130

Zyburt, Corporal (US) H. G. 76

Index of Military Units

AMERICAN

Corps
II 65
Divisions
27th 130
30th 130
33rd (Illinois) 9, 65, 111, 119, 129, 130, 157–8
Regiments
131st Infantry Regiment 9, 65, 66, 120, 124
132nd Infantry Regiment 9, 65, 66, 120, 121, 124, 151
Brigades
65th Brigade 65
Companies
Company C, 131st Infantry 119
OC Company, 132nd Infantry 119
Company F, 132nd Infantry 120

AUSTRALIAN

Corps
I Anzac 37, 47
Divisions
1st 14, 25, 30, 44, 45, 46, 49, 53, 145
2nd 14, 25, 27, 30, 44, 45, 46, 49, 55–6, 110
3rd 14, 30, 32, 50, 52, 53, 55
4th 14, 30, 44, 46, 47, 48, 49, 50, 51, 56, 60, 100, 126, 146
5th 14, 30, 36, 40, 41–2, 46, 49, 55, 89
Brigades
3rd 145
4th 47, 48, 64, 66, 75, 80, 128, 146, 151
5th 13, 29, 102, 110
6th 50, 82, 83, 102, 118, 121, 128, 151
7th 28, 97
8th 38–9, 64
11th 64, 66, 75, 81, 95, 128, 131, 151

12th 47, 48
13th 46, 51
14th 38–9, 107
15th 39, 40, 87, 93, 98
Battalions
9th 28
13th 9, 50, 64, 75, 80, 81, 84, 98, 103, 117, 127, 146, 151
14th 9, 64, 102, 103, 151
15th 8, 64, 72, 75, 77, 78, 80, 98, 104, 105, 117, 126, 138, 145, 146, 151–3, 163
16th 64, 78, 80, 102, 127, 138, 146, 147, 151
17th 29, 52
20th 20, 102, 110
21st 64, 120
23rd 45, 64
25th 50, 82, 83
27th 46, 82
32nd 40
39th 98
41st 52, 64
42nd 8, 66, 79, 101
43rd 64, 76, 77, 80, 81, 82, 83, 84, 102, 117, 145, 148
44th 80, 81, 82, 95, 96, 148, 152
49th 98
55th 85, 87, 88, 113
57th 92
58th 52, 89
59th 40, 89
60th 40
Companies
4th MG 138
58th 90
59th 90

BRITISH
Armies
First Army 21, 36
Second Army 36
Fourth Army 51, 56, 60, 65
Fifth Army 48, 53

Corps
III Corps 51, 90, 120
XI Corps 20
XVIII Corps 140
Divisions
8th 159
39th 35
61st 39, 41
62nd 49
Brigades
116th 35
182nd Infantry 42
RAF
RAF Australian No.3 squadron (AFC) 63, 128, 140
RAF No. 101 Squadron 74

FRENCH
Armies
Sixth 137
Tenth 137

GERMAN
Armies
4th 20
6th 20
Corps
XI Corps 99
Divisions
6th Bavarian Reserve Division 37
13th Division 99, 100
43rd Reserve Division 94, 95, 99
54th Reserve Division of Württembergers 98
77th Reserve Division 100
Regiments
13th 100
15th 100
35th 100
58th 100
Battalions
201st battalion 95
1/202nd battalion 94, 95
247th battalion 98
Companies
13th 100

Note on Cover

The photograph reproduced on the lower front cover of this book is one of the best known photographs of Australians on the Western front.

It shows Lieutenant Rupert Downes, MC, addressing his platoon of B Company 29th Battalion on the morning of 8 August 1918. Following the Australian victory at Hamel a month earlier, the Australian Corps was about to begin the offensive which would end the war.

This image is also reproduced on the Australian Corps Memorial at Hamel.

✦   ✦   ✦

After intensive research, the historian W. H. Connell identified every member of Lieutenant Downes' depleted platoon. From left: Sergeant William O'Brien. Private James Cryer, Private Charles Olive (a Lewis gunner), Lance Corporal Louis Price, MM, Private Harry Phillips, Private Horace Buckley, Lance-Corporal Alexander Craven, Private Patrick O'Grady, Private Timothy Leyden, Private Edward Thomlinson, Private Herbert Davidson, Private Horace Towers, Lance Corporal Thomas Pope, Private John Arlow, Temporary Corporal John Bird, Private Frederick Hall, Lieutenant Downes. Sergeant Price was killed in action on 9 August, Private Olive was killed in action on 30 September, Private Phillips was wounded on 29 August, Private Buckley was wounded on 9 August, Private Towers died of pneumonia on 11 November (Armistice Day), Lance Corporal Pope was wounded on 30 September, Private Arlow was killed on 30 September, Private Hall was wounded on 9 August. (AWM E2790)